Finding Our Way Home

"Myke Johnson's beautiful stories from her own journey illuminate the way to reconnecting with ourselves, each other and the entire Earth community. The practices that punctuate the end of each chapter help embody and guide the path of reconnection. A book to savor, it is also a compelling reminder of the legacy of stolen land and genocide, and of the urgency to face the past as a necessary step toward healing and finding our way home."

Anne Symens-Bucher, Executive Assistant to Joanna Macy
and facilitator of the *Work That Reconnects*

"I work with Unitarian Universalist congregational, environmental leaders across the United States. I am keenly aware not only of my need, but what so many seem to experience as a lack, a daily rift between functioning well on Earth, and Living with All Earth in ways that sustain our core. The messages and ceremonies of *Finding Our Way Home* are as essential, I think, as sleeping. But like sleeping, we try to do without as much as our hearts, bodies and souls need to meet demands in these times. This book is welcome medicine for the beautiful, difficult work and love of our lives."

Rev. Karen Brammer,
UUA Green Sanctuary Program

"As a student of *Naiyantaqt*, I have, over the long journey of my life, come to appreciate the rhythm of the Great Mystery; the wondrous Consciousness, the empowered understanding and meaning of *Manitou*, that exists everywhere and in all living and immobile matter. Such connections are profound, relevant, and mark the passage to the future awaiting the enlightened. I am aligned to such kinships and Myke Johnson is a long-time kinship, a seeker of the Divine, a companion in the awe of the Great Mysterious. She boldly embraces the Divine and her quest to connect with the All-Encompassing Mystery. Her book is the re-telling, the sharing of her wondrous spirit, life, and the path to her awareness. Her book will empower true seekers on this Path of Life, a path she confirms by our friendship and mutual journey together."

gkisedtanamoogk, Maine Wabanaki-State Child Welfare
Truth & Reconciliation Commissioner and author of
Anoqcou: Ceremony Is Life Itself

"Myke Johnson's writings are inspiring, transformative and grounded in the mystic contemplative way of life. Reading her reflections and meditations gives you a deep sense of connection not only to Mother Earth but to her own personal journey. This is a companion book for all that are seeking a simple but conscious choice of living in peace and harmony on our planet with all of creation."

Rev. Virginia Marie Rincon,
Episcopal priest and curandera

"During times of chaos, whether private or public, the human psyche/spirit seeks inner and outer grounding as its home base. Using her own life as a prism of refracted insights, Myke Johnson has created a tool-kit for the rest of us to use in our personal and/or political struggle to survive, and perhaps even thrive. As she shows as well as tells us how to concentrate and tap into our deepest energy and then send it out into the universe in order to affect change, she does exactly that with this book, her own special gift to the world."

Gail Collins-Ranadive, author of
Nature's Calling, The Grace of Place

"In *Finding Our Way Home*, Myke Johnson names the many disconnections that modern people constantly experience as the core spiritual issue of our time. And then through wisely chosen stories from her own experience, she shows us how we might reconnect the inner pieces of ourselves, our relationships in genuine community, and our relationships with the earth into a more integrated whole. She helps us remember our deep belonging with all that is. And that as we engage this process, we are finding our way home."

Rev. Deborah Cayer, lead minister,
Eno River Unitarian Universalist Fellowship,
Durham, North Carolina

Finding Our Way Home

A Spiritual Journey into Earth Community

Myke Johnson

Small Bird Press
Portland, Maine

First Printing: 2016

Author Photo by Margy Dowzer.

Excerpt from "Heart Poem" by Elizabeth Cunningham, *Small Bird: Poems and Prayers* (Barrytown, NY: Station Hill, 2000). Used by permission of the author.

All website addresses are accessible as of November 2016. Due to the nature of the internet, changes may occur following publication.

ISBN 978-1-365-56686-8

Small Bird Press
Portland, Maine

smallbirdpress@mail.com

www.findingourwayhome.blog

For the water protectors at Standing Rock,
and the many other people who are rising up
quietly, persistently,
with no weapons but prayer and love,
to guard and cherish beloved water.
Water is Life.

Table of Contents

Introduction: The Chamomile and Me

When I was a young adult I became intrigued with the use of natural herbs for healing. I read how particular flowers and leaves and roots were able to address different ailments of the body. I purchased herbal products in the local food coop, and steeped them in teas when I didn't feel well. I learned, for example, that chamomile tea was calming during a time of stress. Then one day, with a group of peace activists protesting outside a nuclear weapons facility, someone pointed out to me a chamomile plant growing wild by the side of the road.

It was tiny, easy to overlook, with tight yellow-green berry-like flowers. Its feathery leaves branched out over a stony patch of ground. I suddenly felt the connection. Chamomile wasn't merely something I bought at the store. It was a plant that grew by the side of a road. Something in those chamomile flowers could ease my stress. We were related to each other in a deep, essential way—physically, chemically. And not only chamomile. I understood in that moment I was not separate from any of the plants or animals or people on the earth. We were all one, all interconnected. Something in me woke up.

But if we were one, why did we lose our awareness of our connection? What broke us apart? And more importantly, what could bring us back together? Standing outside that nuclear weapons facility, the contrast could not feel more devastating. If we truly felt our interconnection, how could we even imagine such destruction? Somehow, we had become lost, we had become divided—from the plants, from the earth, from other human beings, from the *Mystery* binding all of us together. How could we find our way back to each other?

When I reflect on my own life, I can trace a pervasive pattern of separation. My family moved frequently when I was a child. I had attended twelve different schools by the end of the eighth grade. I often felt desperately lonely, and frightened about making new friends. It took a long time to adjust to a new place and a new group. What did I lose each time we left another home?

During those years, the Catholic religion offered a kind of solace for my sense of dislocation. I was taught this world was merely a way station, a valley of suffering, on the way to our real home. Our real home would be in heaven with *God*. But there were qualifications: only after we died, only if we were good enough, only if we gave up the joys and pleasures of this world. I embraced those messages with great relief and seriousness, and dedicated my life to that spiritual path. I remember the day I hid in the bathroom—in my large family it was one place to find privacy—and promised Jesus I would become a nun. I was seven years old.

I was taught the spirit was separate from the body, heaven separate from the earth, humans separate from nature. But those beliefs were not unique to me or to Catholicism. All of western culture assumed human beings were separate from nature. People saw themselves as distinct and superior to nature, and considered the earth merely a resource bank to exploit for their own use. Western religious traditions had been an integral part of these disconnections.

Looking back, I can understand my spiritual yearnings as a hope for connection. I was searching for roots, for belonging, for a way to feel my bond with other living beings. Deep inside me, I knew I needed other people, I needed community, I needed location. But no one had taught me it might be right here, no further away than the ground beneath my feet, or a chamomile plant by the side of the road.

How do we find our way back into community with this earth? There is evidence everywhere pointing to the connections between all beings. I look, for example, at DNA, the microscopic genetic code that shapes the forms of living creatures. It was discovered in 1953, the year I was born. With four elements arranged in a variety of sequences, DNA engineers the diversity of all species on earth. And yet, it also reveals our similarity. Human DNA includes elements in common with the DNA for yeast. Even microbes deep within caves—feeding on poisonous chemicals and never entering the light of the sun—these strange bacteria have a DNA code akin to our own. All life, as we know it, is written in the same language.

Our minds are likewise interwoven. Humanity is an inherently social species. Think about language. Human beings speak to each other. I am able to create sounds with my voice, and a certain meaning awakens in your mind. When I say the color *yellow-green*, you can hear the word *yellow-green*, and see it within your imagination. When I say the word *lonely*, you call to mind your own well of feelings and memories. Through language I can touch your mind and heart. Language enables us to create complex webs of friendship and culture. Even with multiple varieties of languages, we can translate from one to the other and communicate across the globe.

How do we find our way back into community with this earth? Even when we wake up to our interconnection, there are still fractures between us. The house where I first lived in Maine was on a beautiful acre full of trees. After we had purchased the house but before we could move in, I came to sit in the backyard. I spread a blanket on the ground, and was quietly listening to the sounds of the birds and the rustling of leaves. A chickadee suddenly flew over my head, then crashed into the glass slider door of the house, and fell to the ground motionless. How could it be that my very home itself was hazardous to these creatures I loved?

Bereft, I picked up the tiny chickadee and held him in my hands. His soft warm body was limp, yet perfect. I sat for many minutes hoping the comfort of my hands might somehow be of help. Then, ever so gradually, he began to contain himself. His eyes became alert and curious. He shifted his feet underneath him to perch in the center of my palm. After about twenty minutes, he flew up into the air and landed on a tree branch. He would live!

It was magical to hold this beautiful creature and watch him return to flight. It was humbling to think I might have been of some help to him. But I also felt incredible grief. How can we be so oblivious to the impact our human lifestyle is having on other natural beings? Human society for centuries has been destroying wild habitats—with our buildings and our mines and our agriculture and our manufacturing and our wars. Now whole species are dying. We are in danger of destroying our own habitat as well. In our time, the environment is deteriorating rapidly and the climate is heating up. Yet governments and corporations continue on the same destructive path.

How can we find a way to live on this earth in a beneficial relationship with all other beings? If we are to have any hope, we need to understand— emotionally, intellectually, physically, spiritually—that human beings are not separate from nature at all. Allan Savory, the founder of holistic land management, recounts a story about certain unintended consequences of separating humans from nature. This was during the early days of park development in Zambia and Zimbabwe. They made mistakes. The valleys had been densely populated with wildlife including buffalo, zebra, antelope, elephant, and lion.

> People had lived in these areas since time immemorial in clusters of huts away from the main rivers because of the mosquitos and wet season flooding. Near their huts they kept gardens that they protected from elephants and other raiders by beating drums throughout much of the night or firing muzzle-loading guns to scare them off. The people hunted and trapped animals throughout the year as well.
>
> But the governments of both countries wanted to make these areas national parks.... so the government removed the people.[1]

The parks set up rules to protect all the animals and vegetation from any sort of disturbance. Within a few decades, however, they were surprised to discover the vegetation had disappeared from miles of riverbanks. They learned that the fear of human beings kept certain grazing animals on the move, and prevented over-feeding that damaged soils and vegetation. With the removal of one species—the human farmers and hunters—the ecosystem had lost its balance. Human beings belong to this earth—we are a part of the ecosystem, for good or ill. We can be a part of the balance as well as a cause of the imbalance.

How do we wake up our awareness to our interconnection? How do we change our lives and our society to become beneficial participants in the earth ecosystem? Who can help us on the path? This has been the journey of my life, and this is the journey of this book.

I believe the journey into connection is a spiritual journey. Since religious traditions have undergirded our division from the earth, we must grapple with religious questions. I never did become a nun, by the way, though I have met nuns who share this journey. Eventually, my path led me into ministry in the Unitarian Universalist movement, where I now serve a congregation in Maine. But the journey into interconnection cannot be circumscribed by denominational affiliation.

I had to learn to put away religious ideas that divide and oppress, and to reclaim spirituality for the purpose of finding wholeness. I learned spirituality is not meant to be a separation from the world, but is rather a felt experience of being connected to the larger reality of which we are a part—connected to the earth, connected to each other, connected to the *Divine*. Without experiencing our connection, we cannot begin to address the dangers facing us in our time.

I invite you to join me on this journey into earth community.[2] I offer stories from my own path, and stories from others who have helped me to find the way. Along this winding road, I had many teachers. Human teachers, to be sure, but also a red bird, a copper beech tree, a piece of bread, a common mushroom, my cats. I have not reached the destination, but I have come to understand a sense of the direction we must travel. We must cultivate deeper relationships with our fellow inhabitants of this planet, both human and non-human. We must understand that the *Divine Spirit* is here with us as well, not separate, but present in each being, and present in the larger reality of which we are a part.

Chickasaw novelist and poet Linda Hogan tells us the purpose of ceremony is to "remember that all things are connected." She says: "The participants in a ceremony say the words 'All my relations' before and after we pray; those words create a relationship with other people, with animals, with the land. To have health it is necessary to keep all these relations in mind."[3]

I hope this book may be a ceremony for re-connection. I hope we can weave new threads across the broken places within our hearts, across the broken places between us and the earth, across the broken places between peoples. I hope we can awaken, we can remember, the reality in which we actually live, the unity of all. We belong here. There is an interweaving fabric in all of life. The chamomile plant can soothe my anxiety. My hands can help a stunned chickadee. Human hunters protect river vegetation. All beings are part of one breath. The Buddhists call it *inter-being*. Monk and mystic Thomas Merton writes, "We are already one. But we imagine that we are not. And what we have to recover is our original unity. What we have to be is what we are."[4]

PRACTICE

At the end of each chapter, or sometimes within it, I will offer an exercise or meditation for you to bring the ideas I have shared into your own practice. I hope you will feel free also to create your own practices from the stories I tell about mine. And so let us begin.

Our biological unity is revealed in the continuous chemical interchange of all life on earth that we know as breathing. Bacteria first began to fill the atmosphere with oxygen, billions of years ago, originally as a volatile waste product. Now, all of us are breathing oxygen every minute of every day. Without oxygen we cannot survive for even five minutes. When we breathe, we bring into our bodies molecules inhaled and exhaled by other beings. This air is common air. These molecules have sailed here from the winds of Africa, or through the tempest of hurricanes in Japan. Lions have roared these molecules; whales have spewed them forth in a fountain above the sea. There is no breathing separate from any other breathing on the earth. Take a moment to notice yourself breathing right now. As you breathe in,

small molecules of oxygen are entering your lungs.
Welcome these molecules of oxygen.
Most recently they may have been released
by a tree or other green plant,
as part of the plant's process of photosynthesis.
They pass through the membranes of your lungs
into your bloodstream;
from there flowing to every cell in your body.
Imagine the oxygen flowing down
into your belly, your legs, your toes.
Imagine the oxygen flowing up
into your arms, your face, your brain.
As we breathe out, the air coming from our lungs
has in it a little less oxygen and a little more carbon dioxide.
This air goes on to be breathed by other beings.
The plants and trees breathe in our excess carbon dioxide
and use it for photosynthesis.
The cycle goes on.
Breathing teaches us we are one.

1: The Magic of Dawn

It was a small red bird who taught me the most about connection to the earth. It began unexpectedly in the winter of 1985, when I was going through a difficult transition. My first love relationship had ended at the close of 1984, and I was deep in grief about that loss. One winter afternoon, sunk in desolation, I heard a curious sound outside my window. When I looked out to investigate, I saw the bright red plumage of a male cardinal. Its song was distinctive and joyful, and its color shown brilliant against the gray Chicago snow. My heart was lifted by its melody. Ever since that moment, the cardinal has signaled for me beauty and hope in the midst of suffering.

On a more recent summer morning, I was sitting on a blanket in a screen tent in our back yard in North Yarmouth, Maine, pondering the big questions of my heart. I was asking, what is my greatest hope? And my heart answered, I hope we find a way to live in harmony with all life on the earth, that our spirits wake up to experience the unity of all life, that we might join in that beautiful dance. But I also asked, what is my greatest fear? My heart answered, I am afraid the greedy and powerful will kill all the trees, pollute the oceans, and destroy the animals and the people. I am afraid humankind is broken beyond restoration, so cut off we cannot find our way back to the unity. And so I was holding all my fears and my hopes in a deep yearning prayer to find wholeness, to find joy.

Then a cardinal started singing nearby, and came to perch on the ground right near the tent. Suddenly I had no words anymore, just gratitude. His presence brought me back into the magic of being outside, the power of being on the ground, the place where my hope is restored. It also reminded me of the perennial magic of waking up at dawn, the time when the cardinal and a host of other birds sing their most beautiful songs. They create together a dawn chorus.

I first learned about the magic of dawn from my Wampanoag friend gkisedtanamoogk. He had told me that the northeastern Indigenous peoples, collectively called the *Wabanaki*, believe dawn is the most sacred time of the day—the name *Wabanaki* means people of the first light, the first light of the sky before the sun rises over the horizon. This time is considered the best time to pray, to commune with the earth and the spirits within the earth. The cardinal's singing re-awakened that feeling of unity and hope.

So you can imagine my chagrin when, five days later, my partner Margy found a small female cardinal dead beneath one of the windows of our house. We always felt upset when a bird flew into a window—we had tried putting up decals of owls and hawks to forestall collisions, unsuccessfully. But we had never found a cardinal before. Margy knew I'd be very downhearted about it. I wondered what sort of message it was bringing, or even what bad omen · it might portend. After we have associated one of our fellow creatures with a sense of blessing, it is unnerving when something like this happens.

I talked to my friend Estelle about what to make of this small fallen cardinal. She reminded me that death is a part of life, brokenness is a part of life. She said, pay attention for the blessing here. I couldn't imagine what the blessing might be, but I burned incense around the cardinal's small body, saved a few of her feathers, and buried her in the composting leaves at the back of our yard. "Thank you for the joy your species has brought into my life," I said, in my thoughts, and I wished her well in the great cycle of life. I asked her to show me what I might learn from her death and her life. I also promised to put hanging streamers around our windows, and to investigate other options to help deter future bird accidents.

During this time, I was reading Leslie Marmon Silko's, *The Turquoise Ledge*.[5] It was a memoir of her days walking the arroyos near her home in Arizona. I found it a slow-going book. At first I was almost bored by it, but once I slowed my own thoughts to match its quiet rhythms, I discovered its revelations. Silko writes about going for walks, and the creatures around her house. She talks about making peace with the creatures who live in the same place she lives—in her case, that included rattlesnakes and grasshoppers. Sometimes creatures died near her house, too, and she felt sad about it, like I felt about the cardinal. In our yard, we had chipmunks and birds and squirrels and toads. Sometimes deer or turkeys wandered through, and neighbor cats. We have to slow down and be quiet to notice the creatures of the earth.

I wondered if the fallen cardinal might be saying: "Stop! Stop pushing, stop trying, stop doing, let go. Be still. Listen. Everything is a blessing. Every day you can go out among the trees right here." Perhaps stopping is a way to pray.

A few days later, I woke early, and heard a cardinal singing outside my window, and that called to me. So I went out again and sat on my blanket and tried again to open my heart to the natural world all around me. When I look at any writing in English, even the tag on the edge of the screen tent, I cannot help but read the writing there. Yet when I looked at the plants or the mushrooms in our yard, I realized I did not know how to read the earth. I didn't know many of their names or their characteristics. Our species has become so isolated, so alone in our own thoughts and works. I wished I had a guide to teach me how to read the earth.

Then I saw a small slug moving slowly through the grass. As I was watching it, I realized the slug was reading the earth, and I wondered what chemical messages it found in narrow trails through the grass. It was on its way toward a mushroom. I took photos of its golden body, tried to pay attention to its slowness and intention as it climbed the mushroom stem. Even a slug can be a teacher. Can I slow down enough to read what the slug can read?

Sitting quiet and listening to the cardinal singing, these words came into my heart: "Whatever you do there is beauty in it: the work, the rest, the prayer, the play, the listening. Awaken to beauty, be present to it, the hidden beauty of the ordinary is like the muted beauty of the female cardinal. Dispel sadness, awaken to beauty and joy."

That July, Mona Polacca, an elder of the Hopi and Havasupai people, spoke at the congregation where I serve as a minister.[6] She talked about how we come into relationship with all the elements of the earth, with water, and air, and fire, and earth. She blessed us with the feather of a water bird. Someone at the talk asked Mona what gave her hope. She said, hope comes with each new dawn.

Feeling encouraged by her words, the next day, I woke up at 5 a.m. and went outside a few minutes later. It was already so light! The sunrise was to be about 5:18. The birds were all singing their morning songs. Soon I could see a red orange light through the branches of the spruce tree. I felt anew the awe-inspiring power of the sun. All plants convert sunlight into energy they can use, and animals eat the plants, and we eat the plants and animals and our bodies are formed of this. You could say that we *are* the sun. Every fiber of our being is created by sunlight. All the earth sings to this light, this star from which we are created.

And even more, the sun is visible to us. We have evolved in such a way that we can recognize this parent—most creatures of the surface of the earth feel and see the sunlight. I felt joined together with that song of the earth, a prayer of thanksgiving to the sun. Thanks for life! I chimed in. Thanks for vision to experience the life all around me of which I am a part, and for hearing and smelling and tasting and touching.

After such a magical moment, you might think I would be awake every morning after that. But it wasn't so easy for me to actually get up at dawn. To sustain it I would have to go to bed much earlier than I was used to. The very next morning I had planned to sleep in, because I was up late the night before. But in the middle of my sleeping, I heard a banging sound.

I stirred, and realized one of our kittens was inside the closet, pushing against the sliding doors. I grumbled, but the clock said 5:15 a.m., exactly five minutes before sunrise. Feeling duly summoned by forces greater than myself, I crawled out from under the sheets, pulled on my shoes, and went outside once more, while the red brightness was just appearing in the east.

Each sunrise is a dance all its own, a scattering of light between clouds and clear sky. This sunrise was a dance of color, of sky turning round through red and pink and orange and yellow and blue. And then, it seemed only a few moments later, the sun disappeared into gray clouds, and the dance became invisible.

Have you ever thought about how the sun doesn't really go up and down at all? How it is actually we on earth who are moving, turning toward or away from our view of the sun? Science has taught us that. The earth spins on its axis once every twenty-four hours, and this spinning creates our day and night. Most of us know this intellectually, but can we feel it?

If I face the east, I am facing the direction in which we are always moving. Here in Maine, we are moving with the surface of the earth at about 620 miles an hour—almost ten times faster than a car on the interstate! In the morning, when I first see the sun in the east, I am actually moving toward the sun, and if I peek over my shoulder back to the west, it is like looking out the back window of a car—things disappearing into the distance. At the end of the day, the sun seems to disappear as well.

It would make us dizzy to be aware of this motion all the time. But for a moment, I can be dizzy with the wonder of it all. Scientific knowledge helps to open up an awareness of reality beyond what I can see with my own eyes, and leads me deeper into a visceral experience of awe and connection. The natural world is the original holy book, the original sacred text. The earliest forms of religion were responses to the mysteries of the earth and sky. As our ability to read this book of the universe grows, our spiritual practices are trying to catch up.

The next day, Margy and I traveled to Star Island, a conference center that is an island off the coast of New Hampshire. It is a rather small island—you can see the water from almost every place on it. It turned out the windows in our tiny room faced the east. The next morning, through my open window, of course I heard a cardinal singing before sunrise. Once again, it seemed to say, "Come outside!"

Right beyond the door of our room was a porch, filled with a line of many rocking chairs, all facing east. I could crawl out of bed wrapped in a blanket, and sit in a rocking chair to watch the sun rise over the ocean. That day, the clouds formed variegated patterns of pink and orange, blazing up through the whole eastern sky. The cardinals jumped from bush to bush close to where I was rocking in my chair.

Watching the beauty of the sunrise during the next several days, I was again thinking about how the sun generates its own energy, how all the stars do that. We on earth are more like children, we are utterly dependent on this light-being for all our needs. All of the energy human beings generate and use all over the earth relies on the sun as its ultimate source. The whole sphere of life on earth is a child of the sun. Yet the sun is so personal too. We can feel its warm touch on our own faces—and that touch changes our body chemistry in deeply beneficial ways.

One morning, I heard the cardinal at 4 a.m. Closer to first light. The waning crescent moon was hung over a deep pink skyline. I began to wonder why we don't always get up with the light. It is actually quite bright in the hour between dawn and sunrise.

Before that summer, I had used the words *dawn* and *sunrise* interchangeably, but I learned *dawn* refers to the first light before sunrise. There is so much of it. Enough to read and write in my journal. We could save a lot of electricity if we got up at first light, and went to bed earlier. Of course, that is the logic behind daylight savings time, when we set the clock ahead so we wake up an hour earlier during the longer days.

But what would it be like if our world was oriented to the rising and setting of the sun? Then every day we'd rise a little later or earlier than the day before. Because the sunrise changes every day. We'd have long days in the summer, and short days in the winter. The earliest sunrise in Maine comes in mid-June, just before 5 a.m. Daylight Savings Time. (That would be 4 a.m. Eastern Standard Time.) The latest sunrise comes about 7:15 at the end of

December, except, because of time changes, it actually gets to 7:22 in early November, before we fall back with the changing of the clocks.

Perhaps it wouldn't be practical, in our world, to plan our day according to the sun. We plan our lives according to the clock. But what do we lose by that? While I was trying to explore the natural rhythm of dawn, I could feel how disconnected I was from all natural rhythms. Rising at dawn was a way to deepen my relationship to the seasons of the earth, and to the sun, and to the birds. But it makes me wonder, "Why do we try to shape the earth to our demands? Why don't we try to shape ourselves to the rhythms of the earth?" And what might happen if we changed that pattern?

Cultures and religions all over the world have honored the sacredness of dawn, the sacredness of the sun. This isn't new. Our word *sun* comes from the Old English *sunne* which was related to the Germanic sun *Goddess*, *Sunna*. It shows up in our everyday language—the first day of the week is called Sunday. Christian monks and Hindu priests rise at dawn; Muslims also, during Ramadan, as well as Indigenous peoples across many cultures. There is something in our human life that wants to be attuned to the life of the earth, that looks for beauty and joy in these simple patterns.

But still, we each have our own personal circadian rhythms. Scientists have found individual rhythms have a genetic basis and are incredibly difficult to change. Their research shows that some people, whom they identify as larks, naturally rise early, while others are tuned to a later cycle, identified as owls.[7] So I am not suggesting everyone should start rising at dawn. I am not even sure if I can shape my life in that way.

I kept experimenting. When the days got shorter, the dawn came later. But then it grew too cold to sit outside like I did during the summer. Sometimes I sat by the window and watched the sunrise from the comfy chair in my room, a tiny black cat curled up in my lap. But I remembered the message of the cardinal singing at dawn: Come outside! And so I would take a walk in the cold, or dress up in snow pants like when I was a child. Come outside.

Here is what I noticed. Whenever I take even one small step toward attuning myself with the larger earth, I feel blessed by it—I feel more beauty and joy. And yet, for each small step, I also feel challenged—aware of how broken off I am. Aware of how broken off we are as a people from this earth that is our whole life. Now I believe this is the essence of the message the cardinals were sending to me, the small fallen cardinal and the ones singing at dawn. Our society has been on a destructive path, which may bring to an end the songs of all cardinals and our own lives as well. If we start to open our eyes, we see that brokenness. But there is also so much possibility for life and joy when we turn toward connection with the earth.

I have to believe awakening to this brokenness and this beauty is essential to the spiritual journey. We cannot have one without the other. My greatest hopes trigger my greatest fears. My greatest fears call forth my greatest hopes. I believe when we enter that place between our greatest fears and our greatest hopes—when we encounter our own vulnerability, and call out for help, something can rise in us like the dawn... and this is the place where *God* lives.

PRACTICE

If you want to feel your connection to the earth,
the first step is to go outside.
If you can, go outside at dawn or at sunset—those times of the sun arising
and departing are particularly powerful.
Then, stop. Be quiet.
Pay attention to what you see and hear and feel
all around you.
Notice the beings that come near to you.
Pay attention to what you feel inside your heart.
Notice your own greatest fears and hopes.
Invite the beings that come near
to offer wisdom for your fears and hopes.
Keep going outside as often as you can.

2: Signs and Contradictions

One evening, during my first year in college, my best friend Lori and I were sitting in the quiet candlelit chapel of our campus. A few other people were also there, scattered about the pews. I remember feeling we each seemed so isolated in our private meditations. I was moved to reach out and take the hand of my friend. Little did I realize, at that very moment, she had been wrestling with her own inner spiritual struggles.

Feeling a certain despair, she had just prayed, "*God* if you are real, I need a sign. It doesn't have to be a miracle; I just need you to touch me in some way." Then, I innocently took her hand, and it was the touch of *God* she experienced.

From my earliest memories, I was familiar with the idea that *God* could touch our lives. I grew up with a father who was a mystic. My father didn't merely believe in *God*, he was in love with *God*. He had called out to *God* and experienced an answer. It filled his life like a contagious fire. A spark of that fire ignited in my heart too.

My father later described to me his own pivotal experience, which occurred when I was about eight years old. He told me that one day in prayer he had offered his life to *God* unreservedly. A few days later he was lifted to a state of spiritual bliss that continued for two weeks. During that time, he could feel no pain, and he said if he went walking in the rain, he literally did not get wet. It was during the time when the Russian cosmonauts became the first human beings to leave the earth's atmosphere, and when he tried to explain what had happened for him, that became his metaphor—he was lifted out of this world. When he read the Christian scriptures, he was struck by the message that Jesus, who had been in glory with *God*, left that glory to become a human being. He felt then, he too should let go of this heavenly state, and come back into the ordinary human world of suffering and joy, so he could be of service. And so he did.

Living with a mystical father was a powerful gift for me. Learning to pray was like learning to talk—there was an expectation someone was listening. *God* lived in our house like another member of the family. *God* was talked about as a source of infinite Love. I experienced moments of being held in the care of a strong and cherishing presence.

But there was a shadow side to this learning, as I have said, beliefs ingrained in my psyche without my even being aware of them at the time. I learned this earthly world was not important; rather, we were meant to leave it behind and join *God* in heaven. When I was lonely because of our family's many re-locations, I used to have fantasies of dying, so I could finally be at home with Jesus. Obedience and self-denial were the important virtues. I learned other aspects of life were less than sacred—my femaleness, my body, my sexuality. On the one hand, none of that mattered. But on the other hand, none of that *mattered*.

My father was good and loving and even playful, but he was not perfect. He was human. He could be angry and sad and disappointed and critical. He was utterly convinced of his own beliefs and he dominated our family life. As I grew to adulthood, there came a time when I realized that just because my father had had an experience of the *Divine* did not mean he was always right. I needed to follow a journey that eventually took a very different turn. My relationship to my father teaches me about the complications of seeking to touch the *Divine*.

When I was sixteen, my parents and I became involved in the Catholic Pentecostal movement, which at first was a very nurturing and empowering community for me. It was founded on the idea that the *Spirit* could directly communicate with each of us and would guide us on our path. I was "baptized in the *Spirit*" and spoke in tongues. I felt *God* speak in my heart, and saw a friend's headache go away when I laid my hands on her head. I continued to be actively involved during my years in college. But then a shift began happening in the community, moving it away from a free-flowing egalitarian process toward a more hierarchical structure.

During a prayer meeting I attended, one of the leaders heard the *Spirit* say men should be stronger leaders and women should be more focused on supportive roles, as it was in the letters of Paul in the Bible. He suggested we participate in a laying on of hands for that male leadership. But the *Spirit* in my heart was saying men and women were equal and had equal gifts to share with the community. I didn't feel strong enough to disrupt the group with a contrary message, so I went to the women's restroom instead. It was the last prayer meeting I ever attended. I felt broken-hearted—I felt I had lost my spiritual community.

My great helper throughout all of this was a woman professor of the Bible, Sister Amata Fabbro, who taught her students about the scholarly interpretation of sacred texts and the dangers of trying to read a text literally.[8] She taught us how culture had shaped the writings of the Bible, and even shaped people's actual experience of the *Divine*. If we sought to understand the messages of the Bible, we needed to understand the cultures in which they were created and how those cultures influenced those messages or were influenced by those messages.

One important example was that every society of the Biblical world was hierarchical: free men held all the power and women and slaves were in subservient positions. So of course the writers of the texts would take for granted such roles. In that context, what was more compelling was they also preserved stories in which the normal hierarchy was subverted, where, for example, Paul writes, "There is no longer slave or free, there is no longer male and female; for all of you are one in Christ Jesus."[9]

I learned that both the heart and the mind are critical tools in our search for the *Divine*. I'd like to think people who have a spiritual experience will always get it right—they will be accurate in their understanding of the truth and full of compassion. But it doesn't work that way. Our experience of the larger reality, the great Mystery, is mediated by our human limitations and our human preconceptions. People with spiritual conviction can be destructive as well as uplifting. Spiritual community can hurt and oppress, as well as nurture and help. I had to leave that spiritual community because it had become a source of hurt and oppression to me. Jesus once said you can know a tree by its fruit. We must pay attention to the fruits borne by spiritual experience, and weigh it all by the light of our values.

When I was twenty-six, I became even more deeply conscious of how my religious tradition had been overwhelmingly shaped by the dominance of men in our culture. Dominance was a pervasive paradigm putting men over women, white people over people of color, rich over poor, humanity over nature, soul over body, heaven over earth. The work of feminist philosopher Mary Daly helped me better understand how social hierarchies infiltrate even our most personal images and experiences.[10] A white male-dominated culture will create within us white male-dominant images of *God*. The King. The Judge. The Lord. The Father. And those images in turn construct the cultural norms by which we live. The male dominated religions had excluded women from spiritual leadership, and even burned them as witches.

Daly's book turned my world upside down. Everything I thought I knew became suspect. I didn't know what to do about *God*. After being at the center of my life, the word became almost noxious to me, and evoked oppressive forces in my life. I also had moments of great anger and sadness at *God* that women had been so abused throughout history. You see, I still felt a relationship to some sort of nameless *Divine*. But I didn't know how to imagine or think about it.

Images matter. The kind of images that fill our thoughts matter. If we imagine the *Divine* as male, that says that males are most important. If we imagine the *Divine* as a judge, that teaches us to be afraid.

My saving grace was to be part of a wide network of women who were wrestling with all of this together. We began to counter the oppressive forces of patriarchal religion by creating new images of the *Divine* in a conscious way. We re-imagined *God* as female, by calling her *Goddess*. We reclaimed female power by calling ourselves *witches*. We remembered that many cultures have worshipped the *Divine* in female form. And we didn't only change the gender of the *Divine*. We re-imagined the *Divine* as inherent within our bodies, within nature, within sexuality, within all the elements of the universe that had been excluded from sacredness.

But is it possible to imagine a *Goddess* and also experience her as real? What is real and what is imaginary? Here's the thing I discovered. The *Goddess* began to feel real to me when my life started to change. Something is real when it makes a difference to us, when it causes transformation. Images become real when they open a door and shape the world. The *Goddess* became real when the power of women became real—when we were able to embrace our own sacredness, affirm our own intrinsic value and dignity, and live out our own gifts and talents and leadership. We moved from taking supporting roles in the stories told by men, to become the authors of our own stories. As the playwright Ntozake Shange puts it, "…i found god in myself and I loved her! i loved her fiercely."[11]

I had learned images are shaped by culture, but it did not lead me to abandon mystical ways of knowing in favor of only the logical and provable. Even logic had been a part of the hierarchy over other ways of knowing— now I tried to be open to it all, to welcome images, rationality, experience, intuition. There are times when experience—our own or that of others—goes beyond our rational understanding. Some non-white cultures are more at ease about such phenomena. I have a friend who is Puerto Rican. In her culture, one of the ancient traditions brought from Africa is called *Santeria*.

When my friend opens her awareness to search for the *Divine*, images from her culture come to life. She sees the spirits of *Elegba* and *Oshun* and *Oya*, with vivid colors and songs others in her culture also report. For example, *Elegba* is known to appear at the crossroads and his colors are red and black. These spirit beings interact with her and have been very significant in her life. Who is to say they are not part of reality, when an entire culture affirms and cherishes them?

My encounter with people of other cultures has made me more open to the mystical elements of reality, and ironically, also more careful. It has confirmed for me how our cultural context shapes our experience, even at what we believe to be the most intimate and personal levels. If, as a child, I felt held in the loving arms of Jesus, was that reality, or was that an image shaped by what I had been taught to expect? Or could it be both?

Let me tell you another part to the story. My Puerto Rican friend fell in love with an intellectual white woman who was cynical about spiritual matters. When they began a relationship, her lover's cynicism was challenged in an unexpected way—*she* began to see *Elegba* and *Oshun* and *Oya* in her inner imagination. She said to me once, "Those Puerto Rican spirits don't care if I don't believe in them. They show up whether I want them to, or not." Just because we use images to open a doorway into the spiritual realm, that does not mean those realms are imaginary. As my young friend had prayed, "*God* if you are real, I need a sign."

When my images and ideas about the *Divine* began to change, something opened up before me. I embarked on a journey that demanded a deeper confidence and a deeper humility. I needed to have confidence to claim my own experience as valid, whether or not others agreed with me. I also needed humility to recognize the incompleteness of my individual spiritual experience and the validity of truth beyond my understanding.

My spiritual and intellectual journey led me out of Catholicism, but I did not leave everything behind. On the one hand, it might be said I was rejecting the beliefs of my father. But on the other hand, it wasn't such a different journey from my father—each of us had been called beyond the familiar, into a new experience of reality; each of us had to trust this inner experience and conviction more than outer definitions. Even though my father and I are worlds apart in the details of our spiritual expression, we can still find a deep connection because of this common experience of spiritual journeying.

There was another important gift I kept from my childhood religion. Through my studies I had found in the gospels of Jesus a powerful message of liberation for all of the downtrodden—that message built a bridge to the next stage of my journey. That message gave me a grounding and a touchstone for the meandering, beautiful, and sometimes confusing path I was to follow in the years ahead.

PRACTICE

Think about your own life journey.
Have you felt touched by a Divine presence?
If so, what images were a part of that experience?
How has your cultural heritage
shaped the ways you imagine the Divine?
What has been the shadow side of your cultural heritage?
What has been a blessing?
Have you experienced a profound transformation
as part of your journey?
By what values do you evaluate your experience?

3: Touching the Earth

There is an old apple tree I love to visit. It lives on a small bluff by the bay in Winslow Park. I first met this tree when we went camping there several summers ago, and afterward, we always chose the campsite near the apple tree. The tree is old and it is hollow. Or, as I like to say, it has an open heart. If I contort my body just a little, I can squeeze into the inside of it.

The tree has a history with human beings. There is a horseshoe embedded in the trunk, from some bygone caretaker. A horseshoe for luck. We go back in the autumn sometimes to gather the apples that fall around it. I have never seen anyone else collect them, and they make really wonderful applesauce. I have taken photos of the tree in all seasons.

Sitting underneath its branches, gazing out at the water, sometimes I imagine what the apple tree has seen in its life. Sometimes I imagine being a tree, with roots in the ground, and branches swaying with the breeze. One year, the leaves on the seaward side were all blackened from the salt spray of a big nor'easter. What must it be like to bend into all kinds of weather?

Henry David Thoreau writes about becoming acquainted with particular trees in the woods where he built his hut at Walden Pond. "...I frequently tramped eight or ten miles through the deepest snow to keep an appointment with a beech-tree, or a yellow-birch, or an old acquaintance among the pines..."[12] There is something wonderful and profound about going deeper with a tree.

It is one thing to *say* we are part of the earth, that we and the earth are one. But it is more challenging to *experience* it in our bones. We have been taught by our culture to think of ourselves as separate from all that. We live in houses that divide the inside from the outside. We think of some things as human and other things as natural. It is a mental leap to imagine ourselves as a part of the larger life of the earth.

The earth is so big and so full of life, it would be impossible to know every beautiful place, every species of flower and fruit and animal and bird. But something comes alive in us when we open our awareness to one tree, or to one special place, or to one other species of animal. Because we are finite human beings, we need to pay attention to the small things, in order to come to know the ultimate things.

We don't have to go to someplace "special" to make a relationship to a place that becomes special to us. Leslie Marmon Silko writes:

> All places and all beings of the earth are sacred. It is dangerous to designate some places sacred when all are sacred. Such compromises imply that there is a hierarchy of value, with some places and some living beings not as important as others. No part of the earth is expendable; the earth is a whole that cannot be fragmented...[13]

If we let ourselves become well acquainted with any place or being, we can discover the sacredness within it, and it becomes a link to the sacredness of the whole earth. Thoreau chose to get to know the few acres around his tiny hut at Walden Pond. We might choose the yard around our house, if we have a yard. Or if we live in an apartment, we might choose a spot in a city park, or a trail in a nearby woods, or a big rock. All it takes is some time and attention. Perhaps a blanket to sit upon. Maybe a compass.

One of the first things I do to connect with a place is to orient myself in space by locating the directions of north, east, south, and west. I face each direction, and remind myself what those directions represent to me. North is the place from where my matrilineal ancestors came in Canada, and where the north star is constant in the night sky. East is the place of the dawn, the rising of the sun each day, and reminds me of the songs of birds echoing through the air. South is where the sun can be found in the winter sky, and I think of warmth and light and energy. West is the place of the setting sun, and also where our weather usually comes from here in Maine, the rain clouds and the thunderstorms. Most of my family lives to the west of me.

Each direction may have different meanings for you. There is a long history in Indigenous traditions of both Europe and North America of honoring the four directions in ritual to create sacred space. The meanings of each direction change in different cultures, but the pattern is widespread.

I don't always need a compass to find the directions—I can pay attention to the path of the sun, or find the north star at night. But my compass has been an important tool of orientation to the earth. By paying attention to where I stand right now, and to what is all around me, I am creating a map within my mind. I remember once, when I was in the midst of many transitions, I would often feel so disoriented the only thing that helped was to go outside and lay down on the actual ground. I could say, here I am, and here is the earth below me. Finding the four directions helps me to feel grounded in a place, to really be here.

I heard once about another practice of paying attention to a small place— by choosing a very small place. You mark out one square foot of earth, perhaps with some sort of string on a few sticks hammered into the ground. Then sit near your square foot, and observe all the life forms you find there. Look for the different kinds of plants—in our yard it would include clover and grass and wild strawberries and moss. Look for the insect life—some of it moving in and out, like bumble bees and flies; other staying close, an earthworm or a group of ants. Take pictures of the ones you don't know, and look for them on the internet, or identify them with a biology teacher or friend.

There are also microscopic life forms in that square foot of soil. Thousands of them. If you are able, get a microscope and check out our hidden neighbors in the soil. It is because of all these living beings that plants can grow and be fruitful. Biologists Jill Clapperton and Megan Ryan say,

> When we are standing on the ground, we are really standing on the roof top of another world. Living in the soil are plant roots, viruses,

bacteria, fungi, algae, protozoa, mites, nematodes, worms, ants, maggots and other insects and insect larvae (grubs), and larger animals. Indeed, the volume of living organisms below ground is often far greater than that above ground.[14]

Another way to enter this sphere of connection is through making a relationship with one other animal. It could be with a cat or a dog. I can play with our two cats, Billie and Sassy, cuddle and pet them, curl up for a nap with them, and we feel love for each other. Sometimes when I am meditating in the morning, Billie climbs up into my lap and sits with me there, purring. Isn't it remarkable we can make a bond across species and communicate in so many silent and vocal ways?

I heard an incredible story about a connection between a man and some elephants. Lawrence Anthony worked with rogue elephant herds in a reserve in South Africa. He had taken on these animals because they were causing trouble in other reserves, and were about to be shot. He spent time living with them, feeding them, talking to them, until finally they relaxed in their new home. He became known as the Elephant Whisperer, and other troubled animals were sent his way.

But here is the amazing part. Mr. Anthony died in March of 2012 and a few days later two of the elephant herds were seen walking slowly, as if in a procession, toward his house. They walked for twelve hours from a distant part of the reserve, and when they came to his house, they stayed around for two days, as if to say goodbye to the man who had saved their lives. How could they have known he had died? Their journey is a testament to the mysterious connections between all beings.

Our modern society is beginning to understand we are not separate from the earth or other beings on earth. In the 1970s, chemist James Lovelock, working with biologist Lynn Margulis, proposed the hypothesis that the living organisms on earth interact with their inorganic surroundings to form one self-regulating, complex system that fosters the continuation of life. He named the theory after the Greek *Goddess* who personified the *Mother Earth, Gaia.*[15]

For how many years have people been calling the earth our *mother*? The image dates to the days before history, in cultures all around the world. Our mother is the one who feeds us. Before we are born, in our mother's womb, we are literally fed and shaped from out of her body. After we are born, we are given milk from her body. The earth is our mother because we are created and fed from her body. We are a part of her, and all of our life emerges from her.

We live in a time when this ancient understanding is coming to the fore again. During the industrial age, people treated the earth and all its creatures as resources to be exploited. Whatever could be mined or cut down or dammed up or harvested was taken for human use. So much was taken and destroyed that now for the first time in history, we can see the fearful limits of the earth's abundance. In order to find wholeness, we must restore a relationship of respect and honor between people and the rest of nature, particularly the parts of nature that give us our life through food.

There is a practice that has grown popular in some spiritual circles called finding your power animal. I think people want to find a power animal because we want to honor our fellow creatures here on earth. We instinctively sense something important might emerge if we can know and celebrate one unique animal. Finding a power animal is part of some old and some modern shamanic practices, but the idea is often romanticized in our society. Various human attributes are attached to animals in a mythological way. People look for the exotic and the wild, and you can even buy a deck of cards from which to draw your animal.

But there is a more authentic way to find a power animal. We can start by thinking about our food. If we eat meat or fish, or eggs or milk, what are the animals that give us their lives, so we can have food? In our society, it is difficult to honor the animals who are most important to us. Chickens, cattle, and pigs are the most widely eaten animals in the United States. Most of them are raised in horrible conditions. When we begin to open our hearts to our connection with other animals, we have to ask ourselves about the animals we eat for food.

I think about the chicken—the animal most eaten in the United States. Sometimes they have been given a bad reputation in our culture—we call someone *chicken* when they are lacking in courage. But chickens lay eggs that feed us, and their bodies feed us. When allowed to roam a yard, chickens will kill and eat the ticks that can cause Lyme disease. They have their own nobility and beauty and give so much to us. A chicken would be a fine power animal. Except perhaps we feel too ashamed of how the humans have treated them. If we respected the chickens, how could we tolerate the agricultural practices that confine them to torturous cages?

To eat is a sacred act. Often, we eat mindlessly. We don't pay attention. When we eat, we take one part of *Mother Earth*, and unite it with another part of *Mother Earth*—our own bodies. Eating is necessary for life, and yet includes death of some kind, whether of animals or plants. The great mystery of life and death can be present to us every single day, in the ordinary communion of eating a meal. But most of the time we are separated from that mystery because we can pick up our food from the grocery store, heedless of the reality that this food is from living beings.

Some people, seeking to give greater respect to our fellow creatures, make a choice to refrain from eating meat. That can be a powerful practice. For my part, I try to honor the sacredness of all beings by thanking the creatures who have given their lives that I might eat. I try to buy meats of animals who have been raised without cages, without chemicals, with some ability to live out their natural lives before they become our food. In our culture, it is challenging, but becoming more and more possible. It begins by making that one simple change—to recognize and celebrate the beings who provide our food at each meal.

The Indigenous Innu people of northern Quebec had traditional rituals in which they asked the *Caribou Spirit* to help them in their hunting. They believed this *Spirit* would lead them to caribou they could kill and eat. After a successful hunt, they offered thanks to the animal they had taken, and made sure none of the bones touched the ground. The being they ate was the being to which they prayed. We can do that too.

When I watch our cats looking at the birds outside, it seems to me they are doing something like praying. We don't let them go outside—we've interrupted their hunting of birds. But they shiver and chatter in excitement merely watching the birds, and it seems very much like deep devotion.

Novelist Barbara Kingsolver and her family decided to take a year eating only local foods—foods they could grow themselves, or buy from their neighbors.[16] In this way, they cultivated their relationship to a particular place, and also their relationship to all the beings, both animals and plants, that provided food in that location. It required a change in how they thought about food. For example, rather than assume all foods were available at all times, they had to understand the seasons for certain foods. They could look forward to the asparagus in early spring and the strawberries in June. They entered deeply into the local cycle of growing and harvesting.

We might not be able to grow all of our food, but we can try to grow some small part of our food. I started with some blueberry plants in our front yard, because I loved the small Maine blueberries I bought from our local organic grocery store. Then I was given some raspberry plants, and put them in another corner of the yard. I don't have a lot of time to garden, but I set up a small raised bed and tried to grow lettuce and kale and snap peas each year. Even this limited experiment taught me how difficult and rewarding it can be to grow food. It taught me the sacredness of the soil, and the interplay of sunlight and water. It has been one more step toward greater connection with this place and these beings who live with me in this place.

We can also deepen our relationship to the wilder animals who share our neighborhoods. The crows, the chipmunks, the squirrels. Who lives in your neighborhood? If you sit outside very quietly, they may wander by. You can learn their songs, their tracks, their habits. You can offer them food or water or help to enhance their habitat. For the birds, we put out sunflower seeds that are loved by cardinals, chickadees, and tufted titmice; suet for the woodpeckers, and thistle for the goldfinches. Some of the birds are around all year long, but in late spring it is a delight to see the travelers again. We put out a hummingbird feeder at the beginning of May, and we put out orange slices and hope for the orioles to show up. They bring so much beauty to our ears and eyes.

When we make a connection with one small part of *Mother Earth*, we are helped to make a connection to the whole of the earth. We are helped to see that we too are a part of the *Mother Earth*, we belong here.

PRACTICE

Think about the animals or plants you eat for food.
Create a prayer of thanks to say before you eat.
Use this one as a start and adapt it for each meal:
Thank you, Mother Earth, for these your gifts.
Animals and plants, we honor you,
—Chickens, lettuce, carrots, tomatoes, potatoes, olive plants—
Siblings whose generosity gives us life.
May our bodies and spirits be nurtured
and strengthened for the work of this day
And may we too learn the way of generosity.

4: Watching in the Dark

When I was a devoted Catholic child, I learned about the saints who had visions of angels or the Blessed Mother Mary or even Jesus himself. I was drawn to the children in Fatima, and Bernadette of Lourdes, and Margaret Mary Alacoque, and Joan of Arc. I wanted to have a vision, too. I prayed for Jesus or Mary to come and show themselves to me and speak to me directly. I believed spirituality should include a holy being coming down from the sky and standing in front of me. It never quite happened that way. Why not, I wondered? Why tell us those stories if we could not have those experiences?

Ralph Waldo Emerson wrote something similar in 1849.

> The foregoing generations beheld God and nature face to face; we, through their eyes. Why should not we also enjoy an original relation to the universe? Why should not we have a poetry and philosophy of insight and not of tradition, and a religion by revelation to us, and not the history of theirs?[17]

A spiritual journey is our search for our own "original relation to the universe." It is our search for our own face to face, personal experience of "*God* and nature." When I was growing up, it seemed only a few special people might have such a personal experience of the *Divine*. But now I believe I was confused about what I was looking for. Let me use an analogy. I was looking for something like a trip to a great auditorium to see "*The Divine*" in concert; but the *Divine* really emerges more like the sound of a tune in one's own imagination.

It reminds me of a story of Elijah in the Hebrew Bible. He was told to wait out on the mountain, Mount Horeb, because his *God Yahweh* would be passing by. Then there came a mighty wind, so strong it tore the mountains and shattered the rocks, but *Yahweh* was not in the wind. After the wind came an earthquake. But *Yahweh* was not in the earthquake. After the earthquake came a fire. But *Yahweh* was not in the fire. After the fire there came a sound like sheer silence. When Elijah heard this, he covered his face with his cloak. He realized in this utter stillness, *Yahweh* was near.

The spiritual journey is simpler than we think. Not to say it is easy— Elijah traveled for forty days and forty nights before he got to the mountain. But it is so simple, if we don't pay attention, we can miss it entirely. I invite you to experiment with me, starting with an exercise I've adapted from the writing of Starhawk, a feminist witch and ecological activist.

PRACTICE

Start by noticing the energy level within you at this moment.
Are you alert? Fatigued?
Calm or tense?
Engaged or relaxed?
Now, sit up as erect as you can without straining.
Notice how the energy level changes.
Now I invite you to breathe deeply,
breathe all the way down into your belly.
As you breathe in and out,
let go of whatever might be on your mind.
Just pay attention to your breathing in and out,
as you sit quietly for a minute in the silence.
Now pay attention to the energy within you.
Do you notice any changes?[18]

The very beginnings of a spiritual journey are in the practice of paying attention to the energy of the present moment.

When we are first born, we see and hear everything around us without definition or understanding. Gradually, we come to assign meaning to shapes and colors and sounds. We say mama, or daddy, or ball, or doggie. We separate the world into smaller objects we can name and grasp. Perhaps we learn about *God* as a kind of separate object we might name and grasp. But once we assign such names, once we divide the world into objects, we sometimes forget to see what is actually before us.

When I was in high school, I took several drawing classes. Our first lesson was to stop drawing objects, and to start sketching out shadows and light. In order to draw, we had to see at a different level from the level of objects. To pay attention, spiritually, is like that. We are shifting our consciousness from smaller separate objects to larger connecting energies.

As we grow older, we begin to understand non-object realities such as the air, or electricity, or heat. We experience the invisible air through clues such as blowing leaves, or the feeling of its force on our faces in the cold, or the tug on a kite as it rises into the sky.

The word *spirituality* comes from the Latin root *spirare*, which means *to breathe*. When we breathe, we are alive. We are in relationship, through the air, to the world around us, to all other breathers of air: all the human beings, all the animals and the birds, all the trees and the plants. It is first of all a very material, chemical exchange. Breathing is life shared among many beings. We have to use our imagination to perceive the air, but if we stop breathing, we die. Breathing might be called the first prayer.

There are many forces of connection so ever present we might never notice them without flashes of insight or the work of science. Another of these is gravity. We expect to remain held to the ground, we are used to the directions of up and down. Let's take a moment to pay attention to the force of gravity.

PRACTICE
As you sit, feel the pressure of your back and bottom
where they touch the surface of the chair.
Notice how your muscles are compressed underneath you.

Notice the heaviness or lightness you experience.
Now, imagine floating up out of your chair
into the air above you.
Try to do it.
(Do you need more time?)
Now can you feel the pull of the earth keeping you attached?
What would it be like if we all floated off the earth
into the vast reaches of empty space?

If we wish to travel a spiritual journey, we need a way to shift our attention, to tune in to the mysterious forces that connect and uphold life, to the larger reality of which we are a part. A method for shifting our attention is called a spiritual practice.

We can't see the radio waves that surround us all the time. But if we turn on a radio, and tune into a particular frequency, we will hear the sounds of music. The radio waves are always there—it is we who need to tune in to hear them. Spiritual practices are the radio tuners that help us to tune into the music of the universe. We are trying to move beyond our ordinary experience of everyday life, into a different channel of consciousness.

Historian of religion, Karen Armstrong, writes about how, in premodern cultures, there were two recognized ways of acquiring knowledge. *Logos*, or reason, "was the pragmatic mode of thought that enabled people to function effectively in the world." *Mythos*, or myth, "focused on the more elusive, puzzling, and tragic aspects of the human predicament that lay outside the remit of logos."[19] How do we access that which we cannot understand or explain by logic? We must shift to the playfulness of the symbolic mind. Mythic language uses story and imagination and drama as a doorway into that which is beyond logic.

The modern world is devoted to scientific reason, and it has lost track of the meaning of myth—in fact, myth is now defined as something that is not true. But in pre-modern times, myth was the common language of spirituality, and helped people to wrestle with the challenges that were not so easily solved by reason. Imagination is one of the mythic tools of spiritual practice.

Imagination can awaken a deeper part of our consciousness than reason, can enable us to perceive the energetic realms.

After I left behind the problematic images of divinity from my youth, I opened my heart to new possibilities. The first new image that came to me was a dancing light, infinitely small. This image evoked the hiddenness of the *Divine* yet also its inner closeness, and ignited a spark of joy and hope. At that time I was working with midwives who helped women to give birth at home. I found in the image of a birth-giving mother another way to encounter the *Divine*, as *Mother* and birth-giver of all life. I was in awe of the strength, devotion, and surrender that were a part of the process of giving birth. It taught me the *Divine*, too, is involved in a process of birthing the universe, connected to us through an umbilical cord of love, and yet also moving us to be fully ourselves.

Any time we invite the *Divine* into our presence, through our imagination, what we are actually doing is inviting our hearts to shift their attention. We are re-tuning our hearts to notice the *Divine* that is already here. The images are not meant to be objects to grasp in our minds, but tools to awaken the connection within us. They create a form that can hold the energies in a certain rhythm or shape. I open a door in my consciousness, to see what my literal eyes cannot. When we open the door, there is something that wakes up, something beyond what we can expect or explain. If we don't open the door, we won't know what is out there, or in here.

The Zen Buddhist teacher Huineng says,

> Truth has nothing to do with words. Truth can be likened to the bright moon in the sky. Words, in this case, can be likened to a finger. The finger can point to the moon's location. However, the finger is not the moon. To look at the moon, it is necessary to gaze beyond the finger...[20]

Words and images about divinity are not meant to be literal. This is why I have italicized any names for divinity in this book. *God—Goddess—Mystery—Spirit*. A small reminder that they are not literal. They are like a finger pointing to the moon. If we spend a lot of energy debating the nature of the finger—what good will that do for us? If we defend the finger, or try to ridicule the finger, or argue about the finger—we're missing the point. The point is that the finger is pointing to the moon. The point is to learn to shift our gaze and discover the beauty and mystery.

One August night, I went outside to watch a meteor shower. I was in my driveway, sitting on a reclining deck chair, watching and waiting. Every so often, I would see a streak of light flash across the sky. But mostly it was quiet and dark. I looked at the Milky Way, and began thinking about how far the stars were spread out, and how long it took for their light to reach my eyes. I was thinking about the fact that the light from these enormous, distant stars was reaching my two tiny eyes in an ordinary driveway in Maine. Suddenly the sky seemed so much larger than I remembered, and I felt so much smaller, an infinitesimal speck. And yet I was seeing everything, and what I was seeing was as large as the sky. How could something as large as the sky fit inside of me! And yet it did. I was a part of the *Mystery*.

If I hadn't been watching in the dark, I wouldn't have experienced the mystery of that night. I had the intention of looking for meteors, but what I found was something beyond my intention. To embark on a spiritual journey is like finding opportunities to watch in the dark, however we might do that— waiting, looking for what we think we are looking for, but sometimes finding so much more.

The goal of any spiritual journey is to lead us into that depth, that place where the known crosses into the unknown. There is a part of the spiritual journey that must be intentional, a practice. We must choose to watch in the dark. But the inner purpose of a spiritual journey is to move beyond the capacity of our own intentions, to discover something larger than what we can imagine—a larger reality, a larger love, a larger *Mystery*.

Let me also warn you about what may come next. If we open our heart to awareness of the present moment, if we watch in the darkness, we may discover within us a kind of inner darkness, a kind of emptiness or hunger. This hunger may feel like a hole deep in our being. But it does not mean we have failed in our search. This emptiness itself has been for me a part of the journey.

It can feel like pain or loneliness, or sometimes like restlessness. It is difficult to sit with these feelings and I am tempted to read a book, or find something else that might fill up that empty place. However, instead of escaping or fixing it, I invite myself to be present with it, to surrender to it. I breathe into the darkness and let myself experience the hunger. I accept the feelings of my heart just as they are.

The Buddhist teacher Kinrei Bassis says the "deepest form of prayer is really just the willingness to be still and let the longing in your heart go out without defining or understanding where it is going…. Meditation is the willingness to let go and learn to trust so that we may enter into this seeming darkness."[21]

When I sit with the emptiness, when I enter it more and more deeply, it may open up into an even darker void. Images can help us find the door, but the night we enter is beyond both human logic and images. Scientists say only four percent of the universe is able to be detected—the stars, the planets, those bright points of light. The huge expanse of space is mostly dark matter or dark energy, unknown to us. What sound does silence make? Is it desolation I feel or a kind of abandon? What happens when our minds are unfolded beyond our thinking and feeling? How can we describe *Mystery*? There are no words. We merely breathe in the night. To this we must surrender ourselves.

And sometimes, the dark void opens into something else. The emptiness disappears, and we dissolve into a larger awareness. The energies of the earth, the sky, the stars, the wind blend together. We realize we are joined to everything. We feel held in the arms of tenderness. We feel we have come home.

This experience of arriving into unity might also come unexpectedly, without any waiting or darkness at all. The *Divine* is funny like that. It surprises us. For me, it sometimes comes when trouble or grief has opened a chasm in my heart and the pain of yearning fills my being to the core. It has been in the lowest moments of my life I most experienced the presence of the *Divine*, holding me in love and connection and carrying me through.

If we want to remain on the spiritual journey, we need the tools of waiting and watching, of being present to whatever we encounter—darkness, silence, mystery, tenderness, anguish, communion. Who is to say which is the journey and which is arriving in the *Divine* presence? We surrender to the breathing and embrace the experience of the present moment.

I think back to the image of the radio waves I spoke about before. All the time, there is music moving through the air but we are unaware of it. However, if we tune our radio to a particular frequency, a whole invisible world opens up to our ears. In the same way, the larger reality, the *Divine*, the *Mystery*, is already here, all the time. We are the ones who need to tune in. An even better image is Wi-Fi or a cell-phone. It isn't just about hearing the voice of *God*, like music in the air, but also about our own voices being heard. We are connected. Someone, something, is paying attention to us, too.

There is another part of the Elijah story that speaks to me. Elijah heard the queen was trying to kill him so he fled into the nearby wilderness. He prayed, "*Yahweh*, I have had enough! I wish I were dead." Then he lay down and went to sleep.

A short time later, an angel woke him and said, "Get up and eat." He looked around, and there at his head was a scone. It doesn't say what kind of scone. Did they have cinnamon or raisin scones then? I like to believe if *God* was thoughtful enough to send a scone, it would be a favorite kind. The angel said, "Get up and eat, or the journey will be too long for you." So he ate the scone, and then he was ready to make the forty day trip to Mount Horeb. My experiences of the *Divine* are like that. In the midst of my challenges, I get a taste of the presence of *God*, like a little scone, so I have the strength to make the long journey.

We might think we are insignificant tiny beings in a vast universe. Why would the *Divine* want to pay attention to any of us, prophets or otherwise? I'm not sure, but I do know there are moments when I feel paid attention to, when I feel seen as if by the unseen. It might be as simple as walking down the road in the morning, and suddenly a feeling of warmth fills my heart, as if a familiar hand had just rested on my back. The Jewish tradition has a belief that what we call angels are the manifestations of *God* into our individual lives. Not huge earthquakes, but tiny sounds of silence that touch our souls. A still small voice. Some might call it synchronicity or serendipity. When I have opened my heart to the *Divine*, the *Divine* responds.

And so I have come to believe the *Divine* might be encountered anywhere—hidden within each person, in each plant or animal, in each sunrise or stormy day, in the ordinary and the spectacular alike. Or *God* might be no *where* at all. It means revelation is continuous and always unfolding. It means words and images like *God* or *Spirit* or *Goddess* or *Mystery* are metaphors trying to describe what is indescribable. The Sufi poet Rumi says, "Just remember, it's/ like saying of the king, 'He is not a weaver.'/ ...words are on *that* level of God-knowing."[22]

PRACTICE

Notice the energy in your heart right now.
If you wish, create an invitation in your heart,
open your heart to experience the Divine Mystery
that connects and upholds all life. Be still.
As feelings come up, imagine your breath
filling and embracing those feelings.
Be present to what emerges in your heart.
If you feel emptiness, breathe into the emptiness.
If you feel joy, breathe into the joy.
If you feel confused, breathe into the confusion.
Be present to what emerges.
The beginning and the ending of spiritual practice
are in paying attention to the energy of the present moment.

And one more note—after an experience of *Mystery*, we must be able to come back to the everyday. We must leave the dark and welcome the mundane. In Buddhism, there is a saying, "after the ecstasy, the laundry." In pagan rituals, they say we must ground the energy. After church, there is coffee. We remember to eat food or have a drink of water. Sanity is being able to switch our consciousness from the mysterious to the ordinary. We are not meant to cling to ecstatic feelings. We are meant to be fully involved in all that life is about. Reports author and teacher, Jack Kornfield, "What became clear is that spiritual practice is only what you're doing now. Anything else is a fantasy."[23]

5: Fractal Patterns

How can a *Mystery* as large as the universe find expression within the smallness of our souls? How can we tiny beings experience the *Infinite*? I found a new way to think about this question when I learned about fractal geometry.

The mathematician Benoit Mandelbrot first coined the word *fractal*, and brought to our attention the possibility of exploring the geometry of the natural world. Fractal comes from the word for broken, and Mandelbrot wanted to explore the rough shapes of nature. Traditional Euclidean geometry could not describe these shapes. Mandelbrot writes, "Clouds are not spheres, mountains are not cones, coastlines are not circles, and bark is not smooth, nor does lightning travel in a straight line."[24] Fractal geometry enables scientists to describe the world through complex mathematical formulas.

Perhaps you have heard of the most famous image associated with fractal geometry, which is called the Mandelbrot set. It has a dark area that looks a bit like the shape of a bug, with a large round spot, and a small attached round spot. But the edge is what makes it fascinating. It is filled with beautiful complex curlicues that continue to be complex curlicues no matter how much the image is magnified. In fact, it would continue through infinite magnification.

But "What is it?" I wondered. I am not a mathematician, but I was curious to see if I could make sense of the connection. If you have math anxieties, I promise you, I am only going to give a simple explanation with ten sentences. You are also welcome to skip the next paragraph.

A Mandelbrot set is a diagram of the mathematical equation, $Z = Z^2 + C$. You insert a number into the equation at Z, and the equation computes a new number at C. Then you start the equation all over again with the new number. But we don't care about the answer. We care about how many times you can repeat the process, with the number you started with. If you can repeat it only a limited amount of times, that number is part of the Mandelbrot set—and it becomes a black dot on your diagram, part of the black spot. If you can repeat it an infinite amount of times, that number is outside the Mandelbrot set. Depending on certain variations, it can be given a different color. Only computers can actually do all of these calculations, but they do them very well, and so we can see the beautiful images formed by the equation.[25]

Why should fractal geometry matter to those of us who are not mathematicians? First of all, it gives human beings a new way to look at the universe. When we can describe something, we can see it better than if we cannot describe it. Because we are better able to see the natural world, fractals enable us to have a deeper relationship to the natural world.

It is like learning to read. In order to read, we need to understand the patterns of squiggly lines that form the letters of the alphabet. And then we need to understand how those squiggly lines are combined in multiple ways to form words, and then sentences, and so on. A person who cannot read may look at a book, and it might seem beautiful, or there might be pictures in it to be curious about, but that person cannot understand what it means. When we learn to read the patterns of squiggly lines, the book becomes a doorway into a whole story, and suddenly we have access to a wealth of ideas and emotions and understandings.

As I have written earlier, the natural world is like a sacred text; it is the place where we search for truth and beauty and goodness. We don't have to understand the world to appreciate its beauty. Even a baby can laugh with delight at the bright colors of flowers, or try to catch a butterfly. But the more we understand the natural world, the deeper our appreciation can be, and the more its mysteries open up to us. Fractals can increase our capacity to read the book of the universe.

Once mathematicians were able to measure and describe the complex patterns in the natural world, they realized that patterns permeate the universe. A fractal is a pattern that repeats itself, from an infinitely small scale to an infinitely large scale. In nature, the patterns and shapes may not be infinite, but there is self-similarity at all levels of scale. A classic example is the fern plant. The pattern in the stem and branches of the fern repeat in the patterns of each branching segment, and of the leaves themselves. Complex entities are created from simple designs extended out to many dimensions.

This has both practical and mystical applications. I learned about one practical application from a documentary called *Hunting the Hidden Dimension*.[26] A group of scientists concerned about global warming was trying to determine how much carbon dioxide was absorbed by trees in the rain forest. They could measure the carbon capture of a single leaf, but how could they count the number of leaves in the forest?

They had an idea. They started by measuring the circumference of all of the branches on a single tree. Because of the fractal nature of the tree, the branches form a regular pattern, dividing at certain intervals into smaller and smaller branches. By measuring every branch, they could determine the ratio between branch sizes. Then they took it one step further. They measured the trunks of all of the trees within a given area.

Imagine it with me. If we walk through a forest we see trees of all sizes—small saplings, huge old giants—there is an endless variety of sizes all around us, seemingly in a random pattern. But it turns out it is not so random. The ratio of tree sizes in an area of natural forest is approximately the same as the ratio of branch sizes on a single tree. There is a pattern to it. And by learning the patterns, the scientists could compute how many leaves were in the forest, and how much carbon dioxide they would absorb.

Now when I walk through the forest near my home, I remember this experiment, and look with wonder at the trees around me. What seemed chaotic and random before, is now bursting with new meaning, full of patterns that start to reveal themselves to me, as I gaze with deeper insight. My experience of the trees' beauty expands, and I feel a growing sense of awe. I find myself looking for fractal patterns everywhere. This new understanding has changed the way I see the world. And it is not only visual. I can feel the patterns in bark with my fingertips, and I start to listen for patterns in the sounds I hear as well. Next time you look at a spider's web, or gaze into the clouds in the sky, watch for the fractal patterns.

Our ability to measure the patterns in the natural world has also given us the ability to create digital worlds that remind us of our own. We can use fractal formulas to generate computer graphics that look realistically like mountain ranges and rivers and forests and clouds. That wasn't possible a few decades ago. Such formulas have been used to design antennas in greatly reduced sizes, which enabled the creation of the next generation of cell phones and other electronic communicators. Fractal geometry is enlarging our ability to create new devices that work better, because they follow patterns that resonate with the natural patterns around us.

But what about the mystical application of fractals? It has to do with that very old spiritual quandary. How can a *Mystery* as large as the universe have any connection with our limited human experience? How can we tiny beings feel touched by an infinite *Divine*? I know I have had moments in my life when I felt touched, when I felt cared for by a *Mystery* greater than myself. But if *God* is infinite, or if the *Mystery* is all that is, how can that be? How can a *Mystery* as large as the universe connect to a being like me, so small as to be almost invisible on the planet?

Fractals have given me a new way to think about this dilemma. We have learned a fractal is a pattern that endlessly repeats itself, from an infinitely large scale to an infinitely small scale. What if *God* is a fractal? What if *God* is a pattern that repeats itself from the infinitely large to the infinitely small?

Here is how I imagine it. The *Divine* pattern is a pattern of life and connection and creativity—it expresses itself in the creative unfolding of the universe. It repeats in the attractions of planets and stars, and in the evolution of life itself. Because fractals continue to repeat in self-similar ways at all scales of size, the same *Divine* pattern emerges at the size of our own human consciousness. We can find that pattern in our hearts, in our personal experience of life and love and creativity. Thus we can find the *Mystery* in our hearts, as well as in the larger whole.

By understanding fractals, my intellect can make sense of what my heart experiences of the *Divine*. It helps me to make sense of the tender feelings I feel, and to welcome this help for the troubles life brings. I feel less lonely, when I feel connected to the *Divine* love. It becomes possible to believe I matter, that I am not just a speck of dust in a vast uncaring universe. I have within me the fractal beauty of the infinite *Mystery*.

Human beings have always used images to help us understand the mysterious. I have spoken of images of *God* that are like bigger versions of human beings: a father, a king, a ruler, a judge, or a lord. But when our understanding of the universe grows more complex than these images, or we are hurt by these images, people are tempted to give up on the idea of *God*. For many people, it doesn't make any literal sense to imagine a huge king up in the sky somewhere. And if our experience of these authority figures has been difficult, their images are more likely to inspire fear and guilt rather than help us live our lives.

To imagine *God* as a fractal pattern, a pattern of life and love and creativity, helps me to be a whole person—to bring together my reasoning and my heart and my spirit. Of course, it is not a new thing to compare *God* to a geometric shape. The Christian tradition has used the triangle to describe *God* as trinity. But while the triangle is a static, simple, and smooth figure, a fractal has multiple dimensions, and infinitely complex variations and expressions. That fits my understanding of spirituality—I believe there are infinite variations in the ways we can experience the holy. As the Sufi poet Rumi says, "There are hundreds of ways to kneel and kiss the ground."[27]

There is a third reason why fractals matter. They teach us *we* matter. Fractal patterns are another way we can see all things are connected. The circulatory system of the human body branches out like the limbs on a tree. The patterns of waves on the shoreline are similar to the patterns of radio waves beaming through space. Even though we are infinitely small in comparison with the rest of the universe, what happens on a small scale reflects what is happening on a larger scale.

Some of these patterns may seem to be unchanging and eternal, but there is also unpredictability in the system. Scientists use the word *chaos* to describe this unpredictable behavior. Without chaos, there could be no creativity, because creativity means the emergence of something new and unpredicted.

Perhaps you may have heard of the "butterfly effect." This phrase was used by Edward Lorenz to describe the impossibility of predicting the weather, despite creating complex computer models that looked at multiple variables. Lorenz found that a small change in the initial conditions would produce large changes when the patterned cycles repeated many times. It was expressed in metaphor as the butterfly effect: a butterfly flapping its wings in South America can change the weather in Maine.

We have creative power as human beings. That means what we do within our patterns has an effect on the rest of the fractal network. We are part of an interdependent web of all that exists. If we change a pattern in our lives, it reverberates through the rest of the web; it ripples out like a stone thrown into a pond. We never really know what greater effect we will have on the future of the universe. We cannot control the ripples that flow out. But we do know we have the power to create more beauty, more love, more truth, and more goodness in the web. What we do matters.

PRACTICE
Take a walk or sit outside.
Look for the patterns you can see
in trees, in plants, in spider webs, in clouds.
Find something with branching patterns.
Find something with spiral patterns.
Find something with symmetry.
Find something that meanders.
Find something with stripes.
What pattern would you imagine for the Divine?

6: The Mystery Seed

Do you remember the fairy tale of Jack and the Beanstalk? When he and his mother are in desperate straits, Jack trades their cow for some magical bean seeds. The bean seeds grow overnight into a vine that reaches up to the sky. He climbs the vine and encounters an evil giant, who eats human beings, but Jack is able to escape with a magical hen that lays golden eggs, and a golden harp that plays by itself. He learns from a fairy that the giant's castle is actually his very own—he is really a prince whose father was killed by the giant. In the end, he kills the giant, and recovers his hidden inheritance.

So what does this have to do with us? The bean seeds enable Jack to connect with who he truly is, and with a larger reality beyond the small cabin he shares with his mother. Within each one of us is something like those magical bean seeds. We are so much more than we can imagine. We might say inside each of us is a *Mystery* seed, a seed of what we might become. This *Mystery* seed is our potential to connect with the larger *Mystery* of which we are a part; it is the *Divine* within us that connects to the *Divine* beyond us, it is the fractal pattern of life and love and creativity. This seed is not only in some of us, not only in fairy tales or kings or saints, but in every one of us.

What evidence do I have for this seed of divinity within each human being? How have I personally experienced this might be so? Ironically, it has been illuminated when I faced situations where people were treated as if they had no dignity or value at all. But something within and between people transpired to bring forth a light that could not be extinguished.

When I went to college, one of my best friends slowly revealed to a few of us that he was homosexual. This was a great torment for him and for all of us who loved him, because we were very devoted Catholics. This was in my Catholic Pentecostal days, and all of us were active in the prayer meetings. According to Catholic teaching, homosexuality was against the laws of nature. Tom would try hard to live celibately, and then crash, and go out and "get debauched." He was depressed and often despaired of his life. I felt a painful contradiction in all of this—I knew he was a deeply spiritual person, so why should he suffer in this way? But I didn't have an answer at that time.

Before I met Tom, in the reality of my youth, it was as if gay people did not exist. When I was growing up, during the 1950s and 60s, I never even heard the word *lesbian*, and *gay* only meant *happy*. I never saw gay people on TV, read about them in a book or newspaper, or learned about them in school. As a girl in a Catholic family there were two possibilities for my life path: I could become a wife and mother, or I could become a nun. I never even imagined the possibility of lesbian.

Tom's dilemma introduced to me a whole category of people who were considered unworthy of sacredness. Gay people were not supposed to exist. And if they did exist, they were identified as unnatural, disordered, a mistake, a problem. African American lesbian poet Audre Lorde writes, "We were never meant to survive."[28]

At that time it never even occurred to me I might have something in common with that group of people. I didn't come out as a lesbian until years later, at the age of thirty-one, after a five-year process of struggle and transformation. I didn't imagine I could be a lesbian until after I had identified and rejected the sexism of the Catholic church and begun the change in which I started to truly value myself as a woman.

Gays and lesbians have often been excluded or disparaged even by those who are closest to us. After I came out, one of my sisters refused to let me stay in her home because she didn't want her children to know about gay people. I received a letter from another sister. She wrote, "I pray for you night after night... Homosexuality is wrong! And as your sister I don't want to lose you to the devil." Her words were those many of us have heard from parents or siblings, or from the institutions of our society.

How much guilt, despair, and shame have gay people carried in our hearts because we were not welcome in the reality defined by our culture and religion? Because we could not see the sacredness within? How many gay people have killed themselves in the pain of that reality? How many gay people have been killed, through the violence and hate of a society that has refused to include us in their definition of reality?

But so much has changed. Now it is hard to imagine I didn't know about the existence of lesbians or gay men. Now gay people are in prime-time television. There are supportive high school groups for Gay, Lesbian, Bisexual, Transgender, Questioning, and Straight youth. My friend Tom eventually was able to embrace his sexuality, and share his life with a long-time partner. In 2004, Massachusetts became the first state in the U.S. to allow same sex couples to be legally married, and in the years since, marriage has been won throughout the whole country.

Even language became transformed. Words like *lesbian*, or *queer*—once painful putdowns—were reclaimed as words of honor. I remember we young activists marching and shouting, "We're here, we're queer, get used to it." And then in 2002, there was an episode of the Simpsons on Fox TV, when Lisa Simpson is watching the Springfield Gay Pride Parade, and listening to that very chant. She says to the marchers, "You do this every year. We are used to it." Maybe it is we older queer folk who still are not quite used to it.

So much has changed. For me, it seems like a miracle—in fact, two miracles. First, I still can be amazed I exist as a lesbian at all. How did I cross over into a whole new reality? It is as fantastical as Jack climbing a bean stalk into a castle in the sky. Second, it is remarkable that we who are queer can celebrate being queer. How did we go from being outcasts, to celebrating and believing in ourselves? How did we go from being outcasts, to demanding that reality make a place for us? To celebrate ourselves as queer we often have had to risk every other valuable thing in our lives. We've risked family, friends, jobs, safety. Yet this thing which was considered a problem became the "pearl of great price,"[29] as the gospel says. This heavy burden became the hen that laid golden eggs. And it has been incredible to see!

What happens within people that they can claim the power to celebrate themselves? Police had raided the gay bar, the Stonewall Inn, many, many times, sending its patrons to jail. But in the early morning hours of June 28, 1969, the drag queens started fighting back, and others joined them. The crowd started chanting, "Gay Power, Gay Power." The Stonewall rebellion continued for five days, and was completely ignored by the media, but it was one spark that energized the modern GLBT movement.

What happens inside people when they refuse the rejection of society, and claim the right to name themselves valuable. When people who have been told all their lives "You are no good," find within themselves a different voice that says, "You are sacred." To me, this is powerful evidence of the divinity within us. And this is the premise of the work of those who call themselves Liberation Theologians: the *Divine* is revealed in the struggle of oppressed people for liberation.[30] It is the *Mystery* seed within us growing like a vine into the sky.

Gay people couldn't have done it without the foundations laid before us—all the great liberation movements of this last century. I am reminded of that powerful moment in the sixties when the rallying cry for African Americans became "Black is beautiful!" They claimed the power to name what was valuable. They claimed the power to celebrate themselves. They went from being the second-class players in someone else's drama to being the stars of their own lives. And it was like wildfire sparks lighting up so many more transformations among the ragged communities of outcast people.

That is what happened for me, too. Within a community of women, I experienced a new reality coming into being. With women who were celebrating lesbian existence, I encountered the *Divine* in a new way. Sometimes we called it the *Goddess*. Sometimes we had no name to describe it. But we felt a sacred and holy power when we seized the courage to embrace the body of another woman. Everything shifted. It no longer mattered whether we were welcome at the table of the society that excluded us. We were in a new reality and could no longer be denied.

A friend of mine heard a story while she was visiting Ireland. A short time before, an airport had been planning to build a new runway. On the proposed site of this runway there was an old hawthorn tree. The people in that area understood it to be an ancient fairy tree. Unfortunately, the airport managers didn't care about this: they made plans for it to be removed. However, when they tried to hire someone to do the job, none of the local workers was willing to cut it down.

Still thinking like a corporation, the airport managers decided to bring in outside workers. The workers arrived, and one man gathered some of their equipment and started out toward the tree. As soon as he got close to it, he tripped and fell. The other workers found him gripping his right arm in pain. It was broken. His buddies brought him into the local hospital for treatment, and then abandoned the job and went back to their own town. The airport managers decided to change the plans and move the runway. The fairy tree was not cut down.

Could it be the tree actually was a fairy tree? Or did the beliefs of the people make it so? I remember watching the movie *Peter Pan* as a child. There comes a moment when the tiny fairy, Tinker Bell, having drunk the poison intended for Peter, begins to fade and die. She tells Peter that she can get well again if children believe in fairies. Peter appeals to all of us in the audience, "Do you believe? Clap if you believe!" Clap if you believe in fairies. Perhaps, like Tinker Bell, fairies cannot exist in our reality unless we believe in them.

Queer people have more in common with fairies than merely the epithet gay men are sometimes called. Those of us who exist at the edges of reality have learned reality is not an immutable and solid thing. Reality is capable of being turned inside out and upside down. There are more realities than we know, not only what we can already see. But reality is definitely linked to what we believe in. I couldn't find a way to exist as a lesbian until lesbian women began believing in each other. Until we celebrated our unique difference, rather than trying to get rid of it.

There is power and mystery in difference. Think about the diversity of life on earth. All of life, every species of plant and animal, from virus and bacteria to the largest whales in the sea, are formed from the same inner codes of DNA, a four-letter alphabet. But that DNA spells out billions of different words. According to evolutionary theories, the diversity of life grew from small mutations in the code, happening just once in a million times. One science documentary described them as small spelling errors. That caught my attention. All of the diversity of creation sprang from small spelling mistakes.

In the tale of Jack and the Beanstalk, his mother berated him for the mistake he had made in selling their cow for some worthless bean seeds. But the mistake transformed their lives. It reminds me of the rugs made by the Navajo, or *Dine*, people. It is traditional for Dine weavers to purposefully leave a small flaw in each rug. The Dine understand this as a way of expressing respect, that only the *Creator* can make perfect things. But the meaning I was wondering about was different. If the great diversity of creation is born of the small flaws, then perhaps it is the *Creator* herself who causes so-called "mistakes" to come into being. The mistakes themselves are sacred and holy. The mistakes are the seeds of the next new thing.

One autumn several years ago, I was on retreat with other ministers, and our retreat leader was Rev. Ray Tetrault. He was known to us as a passionate advocate for social justice. Our task together was to reflect on the politics of our time, in light of our role as spiritual leaders.

He started us off with an unlikely reference from the Christmas gospel of Luke. Luke tells us a census was called during the time when Herod was the king of Judea, Augustus was Caesar of the Roman Empire, and Quirinius was the governor of Syria.[31] Ray reminded us they were the politicians in charge of the regional and imperial governments some two thousand years ago.

"But what was really going on?" he asked. Something mysterious. In a small town, a baby had just been born—we know him as John the Baptist—and something new was beginning that would transform the world. This new thing emerged, not from those at the top, but from underneath, from an unexpected and hidden place.

Since our retreat was happening right before the national elections, all of us were sitting there with many stirred-up feelings about the issues facing our country. It would have been typical for us to talk together about our concerns and our analysis of the politicians who would be up for office. But Ray invited us instead to be silent, to listen deep in the quiet of our hearts, underneath our thoughts and feelings. He invited us to reflect on the question: "What is really going on?" What else might be happening here in our own time and country, underneath, unseen, and yet full of potential significance? What is really going on?

We kept the silence for an hour, and then we shared from our hearts. The next day we went back into silence, and then shared again from that deeper place. Ray invited us to move beneath the turmoil of politics, beneath the struggle of winning or losing elections, to the place where all that we value finds its roots. He called it "latent divinity." I knew he meant what I have been calling the *Mystery* seed. Latent divinity is that spark of the sacred, hidden inside each of us, burning like a glimmer of light and beauty and possibility.

The German mystic, Meister Eckhart, writes, "…the seed of God exists in us.... Pear seed grows up into pear tree, nut seed grows up into nut tree—God seed into God…"[32] What might we do together if we remembered each of us has the seed of *God* inside?

In the silence of the retreat, I could feel that spark in my heart, that *Mystery* seed of life and love. I could imagine that seed of divinity in every person alive, pulsing to grow, laboring to be born, and I realized just a glimpse of how beautiful we are. It was that latent divinity that helped queer people to claim our own value. It was that latent divinity that gave Tom the courage to embrace his path. It was that latent divinity that fueled the civil rights movement, and the struggle for women's equality.

Each one of us is like Jack with his magical bean seeds. A seed doesn't look like much. We have to plant those seeds, let them break apart, tend them, and help them to grow. Each one of us has within us this *Mystery*, this possibility for transformation, for changing the world.

What is really going on right now? Underneath the rhetoric of politicians or the maneuvering of nations, something mysterious might be coming into existence, out of the public eye, at the level of the seeds under the ground. In this place of mystery, we are all connected, and anything is possible. In this place of mystery, there is hope for the problems facing our world.

PRACTICE

Sit in silence.
Ask yourself, what is really going on?
What is going on underneath the turmoil of our world?
Sit in silence some more.
Ask yourself, how might you live differently,
if you believed you had the seed of God inside you?
Sit in silence some more.

7: Dreaming in Circles

It is said if a group of people sleep arranged in a circle—heads at the center and feet out like spokes—they create a dream circle. Two or more people in the group may have the same dream at the same time. I tried this once with a group of friends, but I must confess, it didn't really work for me. Mostly I just had a rather poor night's sleep.

But I like the metaphor. The word *dream* can be used to describe both our strange nighttime adventures and also our waking hopes and visions for our lives. We cannot accomplish our dreams when we are separated from one another. Dreaming in circles is about sharing those waking dreams, entering into the magic that can happen when we join our visions together. When we dream in circles, anything is possible.

Have you ever felt on the outside of the circle? When I was in third grade, I went to a new school in the middle of the year. It was a Catholic school and when I arrived everyone was in church waiting for morning Mass. I went into the church but I had no clue what to do next. Everyone seemed to be sitting in groups by classes, but I didn't know where I belonged.

I tentatively edged down into one pew, but the child next to me said, "This is for fifth graders, you don't belong here." I tried to move to another spot without being noticed. Again, the child near me looked askance: "You're not a sixth grader!" I moved to yet another pew, with similar results. I was scared and embarrassed and out of place: I didn't know where to go. Finally, one of the teachers noticed me, and brought me to the pews for the third graders. I still didn't know anyone, but at least I had a place to sit.

Because of my family's frequent moves, questions rose up in me, and stay with me to this day. How do we know if we belong or if we do not? What must we do to belong? Who belongs? Those experiences of dislocation awakened in me the importance of community. Activist Mab Segrest writes about a South African word that describes our essential need for community: *ubuntu*. "*Ubuntu* translates as 'born to belonging.'"[33] *Ubuntu* means our human dignity and fulfillment is dependent upon our links to each other in community.

In contrast, in much of our modern American society, dignity is considered to be attached to individualism. John Locke formulated a theory of society as a contractual type of relationship freely entered into by individuals. Locke proposed that in the original state of nature, all humans were free and autonomous individuals, and from that state, they agreed to give up certain aspects of their independence, for mutual benefit and protection.

But Segrest challenges that individualism:

> [It was] after watching Barbara give birth to our daughter, Annie, …that it occurred to me the degree to which this Original Individual was a ridiculously transparent male fiction. None of us start out as individuals, but as fusions of sperm and egg, embedded and growing in the mother's body for nine months. For months after birth, our consciousness is still merged with its environment, and a sense of the particular and separate self emerges only gradually.[34]

This insight resonates with my experience: we start out in relationship, and our unique individuality grows out of that circle of relatedness. Not the other way around.

But how did our society lose that sense of the circle? Segrest ponders the effect the institution of slavery has had on the self-understanding of white people in America, drawing from the experience of her own family.[35] She suggests in order for a person to own slaves a kind of spiritual anesthesia had to develop, a cutting off of compassion and connection. Though it was not to be acknowledged, many of the children born into slavery had been fathered by the owner of the plantation. What did it do to a man's soul to sell his own children? White people had to deny their relationships, cut off their emotions, and numb their spirits, to maintain this horrible institution for four centuries. She proposes the emphasis on individualism in America is an expression of our spiritual distress.

Even for those whose families were not directly involved in the institution of slavery, the racial dividing lines and patterns have been persistent in our social covenant and imposed on the newcomers and immigrants who arrived here. When our families carry a generational history of separation or oppression, it numbs our awareness of the larger circle to which we might belong. We become so used to thinking of ourselves as separate, we barely notice the diminishment it has caused in our souls. But when our hearts are cut off from the circle of relatedness, our capacity for spiritual depth is truncated. We are not fully alive without each other.

When I was ten, my three younger sisters and I all got chicken-pox at the same time. My mom helped to keep us entertained at home (except for the baby who was four) by playing with us the board game Monopoly. My sister Nita and I became great little capitalists, and played the game to win. We would try to get as many properties and houses and hotels as we could, so we could charge huge rents when the other players landed on our spots. The goal was to bankrupt the other players until one of us was the last player in the game.

But my mom and my sister Vonnie had a totally different approach. They were tenderhearted, and didn't want anyone to have to leave the game. So if someone was about to lose all their money, my mom or Vonnie would loan them some of their own Monopoly money to keep them in the game.

I remember this now and think—what a picture in miniature of the conflict of values in our larger society! One message we learn, even as children, is to try to get as much as we can, and try to win out over all the other people. Compete and accumulate and dominate. But my mother was bringing us another value, the value of mutual connection. She wanted to keep all of us at the table, so everyone had a good time while we played our games.

Her sense of inclusion, and her alignment with the underdog, was reinforced for me in my early spiritual practice of reading the Christian gospels. It seemed to me the central message of Jesus was to care for one's neighbor and even one's enemy—especially those who had little. No one could be excluded from the circle of love. Feed the hungry, give drink to the thirsty, clothe the naked, visit the sick and those in prison, bury the dead.[36] Even though our society claimed to be Christian, I couldn't see those values expressed in our economic or political structures. When I became a young adult, I searched for a way to actually live by the teachings of the gospels.

A door opened up for me when I learned about the Catholic Worker movement. Catholic Worker volunteers live in houses of hospitality to serve the homeless and poor while also working for larger issues of peace and justice. I visited the original Catholic Worker house in New York, and then I moved into the Abrahamic Community in East Lansing, Michigan. It did not call itself a Catholic Worker house, but it followed that model in an interfaith way, and was a part of the informal network of Catholic Worker houses. I met my first partner Gary when he came to help out at the house, and later he and I started a Catholic Worker house in Grand Rapids, Michigan; four years after that, we moved to Chicago to take over leadership of a house for a couple who were moving on. All told, I was involved in that life for seven years.

Dorothy Day was the founder of the Catholic Worker movement, back in the 1930s. There are many stories that give a sense of the spirit she brought to the work. Tom Cornell tells about

> a well-dressed woman who visited the Worker house one day and gave Dorothy a diamond ring. Dorothy thanked the visitor, slipped the ring in her pocket, and later in the day gave it to an old woman who lived alone and often ate meals at [the house.] One of the staff protested to Dorothy that the ring could have been sold at the Diamond Exchange and the money used to pay the woman's rent for a year. Dorothy replied that the woman had her dignity and could do as she liked with the ring. She could sell it for rent money or take a trip to the Bahamas or she could enjoy having a diamond ring on her

hand just like the woman who had brought it... "Do you suppose," Dorothy asked, "that God created diamonds only for the rich?"[37]

Dorothy looked for the treasure in each person who came through the door. She took seriously the latent divinity within each person.

In the great Dostoyevsky novel, *The Brothers Karamazov*, a wealthy woman comes to seek advice from a holy and renowned priest, Father Zossima. She is anxious about eternal life, and wants to know how she can be sure of it. Father Zossima tells her there is no proving the existence of *God* or eternal life. But there is one way she may be convinced of it. "How?" she asks. "By the experience of active love." he replies. "Strive to love your neighbor actively and indefatigably. In as far as you advance in love, you will grow surer of the reality of God and of the immortality of your soul."[38]

The woman goes on to tell him she loves humanity, so much in fact, she dreams sometimes of leaving her privileged status to nurse the afflicted and bind up their wounds. But then she worries if the patients did not respond with gratitude, if they were rude or abusive, she would be incapable of continuing to love them.

He replies,

> I am sorry I can say nothing more consoling to you, for love in action is a harsh and dreadful thing compared with love in dreams. Love in dreams is greedy for immediate action, rapidly performed and in the sight of all. Men will even give their lives if only the ordeal does not last long but is soon over, with all looking on and applauding as though on the stage. But active love is labor and fortitude, and for some people too, perhaps, a complete science.[39]

Dorothy Day would often repeat the pronouncement of Father Zossima, "Love in action is a harsh and dreadful thing compared to love in dreams."

It was not easy to love each person who came through the door. I don't think I could have done it without the support and example of the other volunteers in the houses. Our community life built up a reservoir of compassion in each of us that spilled over to the homeless persons who became our guests.

I remember one night I was sleeping in my shared room on the third floor, alone because my usual roommate was away. Suddenly, I woke to the presence of a very drunk man standing by the side of my bed. Even though I was afraid, something possessed me to respond to him in the spirit of our hospitality, and I stood up, and asked him if he was looking for a place to sleep. I led him to the second floor where there happened to be a spare bed for the night. He fell into it and was soon snoring. Afterwards, I went down to the first floor, a bit shaken up, and woke one of the other volunteers. But all was well, and it was deeply transforming to have experienced the power of active love in a situation that had stirred up all my fears.

In our society, the bonds between people are frayed, and we can get stuck in isolation and competition. There are people who have no one with whom to share their real feelings. To dream in circles means to choose connection, to choose love, to join hands with one another, to find the people with whom we can cast our lot to manifest *ubuntu* in our lives.

It is a spiritual practice to make a choice for community. When we practice loving a particular group of people, we are letting the reality of the universe enter our hearts—we are learning how to experience the reality that we truly are all part of one another. We are learning to experience the divinity within that bond.

Of course we don't usually get it right. Otherwise, we wouldn't need to practice. We are not here to try to fix everything in order to create some sort of perfect circle—we are the circle right now, trying to wake up together. There will be people in any community who inspire us. And there will be people in any community who rub us the wrong way. Those irritating people are sometimes the ones who are the biggest blessings for us.

I caught a glimpse of this one time when I was flying on an airplane, returning home from an event in Washington, DC. I had settled into my window seat, and started to read a book. I can't remember now what the Washington event was or what the book was, but something had inspired me to be pondering this connectedness of all beings, this divinity within all beings.

Then, two young men climbed into the seats next to me. The man in the middle leaned his head against the back of the seat and closed his eyes. A short time into the flight, he started to be sick—his friend gave him a paper bag, and he vomited, mostly into the bag, but also splashing on to his friend. I was a little horrified, and imagined them with hangovers from some drinking and partying.

But then it struck me. If I truly believed in the connectedness of all beings, I would realize these men were my brothers. They were part of me, living in another lifetime, another journey. Something shifted within my heart. Instead of judging them, I was able to feel compassion. We didn't go on to have a long conversation—I just asked, are you okay? I remember a flight attendant coming by to check, and asking me if I wanted to change seats. But I said no. I was experiencing something deeper, something taught to me by these unlikely teachers.

I know a story about a rabbi who was the leader of a spiritual community. There was one member who always gave the rabbi a hard time. The other members of the community hated it. After many years, this person died. Many people were secretly relieved they wouldn't have to put up with him anymore. But the rabbi wept at the funeral. When they asked him why, he said, "That man was the only friend I had. Here I am surrounded by people who revere me. He was the only one who challenged me. I fear that with him gone, I shall stop growing."[40]

To choose community does not mean always agreeing with everyone, or refraining from speaking our own truths. It does not mean we accept abuse, or let people walk all over us. Community includes challenging each other, arguing with each other, and sometimes saying no. But we don't write each other off, we don't speak disparagingly of one another, we don't give up on each other. We treat each other as if we were treasures to each other. Because that is what we are.

I am reminded of one of my favorite stories about heaven. Everyone was gathered around the pearly gates, waiting for judgment day, when a rumor started going around.

"Did you hear that *God's* going to let everybody into heaven?"

"You mean, whether or not you followed the commandments?"

"That's what I heard! Even murderers and heathens!"

Some people started griping, "I've worked hard to be good all my life! I don't want to be thrown in with sinners!"

Others complained, "I can't believe he's going to let in the perverts and the terrorists!"

Finally, *God* showed up. And sure enough, everyone was welcomed into heaven. But a few proclaimed, "We're not going in with sinners and heathens!"

So they were the only ones who remained outside.

Choosing community is a form of spiritual practice because it opens us to that which is *Divine* within our neighbor. What has been hidden is revealed by the light of love. We come to realize we are not alone. We are surrounded by family. The *Divine* light is shining in the threads between us, and deep within each person. Dostoyevsky says: "If you love everything you will perceive the Divine Mystery in things."[41]

PRACTICE
To begin the spiritual practice of community,
you need to risk participating in some sort of group of people.
It could be a religious congregation,
or a spiritual practice group,
but it doesn't have to be focused on that.
It could be an activist group, or a service-oriented group.
It could be volunteering at a soup kitchen or homeless shelter.
It could be a group to discuss the spiritual journey.
Find a group that inspires you in some way.
As you participate in the group:
Cultivate an attitude of curiosity and respect.
Let yourself choose to be glad each other person is here,
to assume they belong here,
and to revere them as a unique expression of latent divinity.
Listen, and be open to the insights the other might offer,
especially when they are different from your own.
Let the process of dialogue expand your own viewpoint.

Assume even when someone is acting badly,
they are doing the best they can do at the moment.
Practice being patient with the irritations that arise in you.
They are often a doorway into learning and growth.
Watch for the magic that happens
when we approach our fellow beings with reverence.

8: Threads of Interconnection

All around us, like a choreography of dance, like a vast symphony orchestra, the beings of the earth move in harmony, in one earth community. I began to notice it most profoundly during one springtime here in Maine.

The forsythias were the earliest to flower, the first week of April. A few days later, I saw a solitary daffodil begin to break through its luminescent green casing. By evening it had opened up pale yellow to reveal an orange center. The next day the rest of the daffodils in our front yard began to bloom, and the first bright yellow dandelions popped open behind the house. I kept taking short walks around our yard and down the street to see what would happen next. The small wild strawberry flowers. The leaves of the violets appearing out of the bare ground where I thought they might have perished in the fall. The green buds of bushes opening into curled leaves. And then, the first fiddleheads of the ferns began to poke through the ground that a day ago had been fern-less.

This awakening seemed to happen all at once. One week there were bare branches and brown grasses, and then suddenly everything was green and lush and colorful. How did they know to come alive all in the same few weeks? It reminded me of what I have read about evolution—that species co-evolved with each other. That flowers emerged along with their pollinators, and each flower with its particular pollinator, so interdependent we do them a sort of injustice to think of them as separate entities.

And of course, in that spring, the insects also came out with the flowers, small ground bees hovering over the grass as if waking from a long sleep. The hummingbirds arrived when the pink flowers of the viburnum opened near our kitchen window. The viburnum buds were the signal for us to put out the nectar feeder, so we humans could be part of this dance.

In those particular weeks of the year, in that beautiful season of awakening, I could see it and hear it and smell it and feel it. If we pay attention, we can feel the threads of interconnection that make of many beings, one indivisible whole.

Vietnamese Buddhist teacher Thich Nhat Hanh invites people to do a thought exercise, to begin to grasp with our minds these invisible connections, this symphony of the larger unity.[42] He suggests we start with an object—it could be any object—and then look at what has conspired in order for this object to be here. He talks about a table, but I would like to adapt this exercise and start with a piece of bread.

PRACTICE

I invite you to find a piece of bread and hold it in your hand.
Then, let yourself imagine with me all that has enabled this bread to be here in your hand.
First of all, think of the wheat. In order for it to grow,
it needed topsoil, with its fungal and bacterial components,
its minerals and small worms.
It needed the decomposition of the plants of many years,
decades, and even centuries to create this fertile soil.
Imagine the sun that shines on the earth, and the rain that falls,
and the earth itself turning round in its orbit of seasons,
and the moon that shapes the tides and the weather,
all utterly necessary.
Think about the wind, which helps the plants to self-pollinate,
and the ancient peoples in the Middle East who began to cultivate the grain
during the seventh pre-Christian millennium.

Think of those who developed it and carried it to many continents through
the intervening centuries.
The wheat used in bread co-evolved with human beings,
and does not thrive in the wild without human intervention.
If your bread is made from organic wheat,
it doesn't use petroleum for fertilizer,
but it took petroleum in the form of gasoline to harvest it
and ship it to the bread makers.
Non-organic wheat uses even more petroleum.
Petroleum is created from the remains of ancient plants,
so this bread is also dependent on them.
Think about the metal in the trucks that drove the wheat,
and in the machines that mixed the bread,
and the mines it came from
and the factories where the machines were made.
Call to mind the yeast, and the process by which
human peoples discovered and developed the properties of yeast
to raise the dough of bread.
Remember the honey, and the bees that work tirelessly to make it, and the
flowers and their nectar.
Remember the water that enabled these ingredients
to be blended together.
Think about the fuel to heat the ovens.
Call to mind the farmer, and the miner,
and the bread-maker and the factory worker;
the food they needed to eat, and the clothing they needed to wear
in order to do their part of the work
that brought this bread to your hand.
The trucker, the grocery stocker, the clerk. The houses they live in, their
schools and their doctors and their dentists.
Think about their parents, and their grandparents
and their great grandparents, and what kept them alive,
to bring forth their children,
that these people who work might be here today.
If you are holding organic whole wheat bread,
think about the growing environmental consciousness
that created a market for organic whole wheat bread,

after many farmers, bakers and corporations
had abandoned the old methods for the appeal of soft white bread.
We could keep going all day to follow all the threads of connection linked to
this one piece of bread.
Paraphrasing what Thich Nhat Hahn would say:

> *If you grasp the bread's reality then you see that in the bread itself*
> *are present all those things which we normally think of as the non-*
> *bread world. If you took away any of those non-bread elements and*
> *returned them to their sources...the honey to the bees, the metal to*
> *the mines, or the farmers to their parents... the bread would no*
> *longer exist. A person who looks at the bread and can see the*
> *universe is a person who can see the way.*

Now, seeing that all non-bread reality is also in the bread,
I invite you to eat the bread,
knowing you are putting one form of the universe
into another form of the universe.

If all of the universe is inherently one unity, what might that mean for our understanding of the *Divine*? People often imagine that *God*, however we envision *God*, is separate from us, that we can think or not think about, believe or not believe in, pray or not pray to that *God*. But if we take seriously what Hanh is saying, perhaps there are no truly separate things, there is no separate self or separate *God*—rather, our "own life and the life of the universe are one."[43]

As part of her memoir, *Working on God*, journalist Winifred Gallagher heard about a Zen experience, called *kensho*, which is a sudden, ecstatic transformation of a person's perception of reality. She records one practitioner's account:

> For some reason, he recalled the roshi saying "Keep your eyes open or you will miss it!" Suddenly, he wrote, "the teacup in front of me seemed to 'fly apart' and all the constituent matter in the cup, and in my body, and in the universe, were the same from all past to all future for endless time. I saw that what seems to be me or a cup is only due to where my self was sitting. This experience totally freed my self

from the coming and going and caused the greatest gratitude to well up in my heart."[44]

Alice Walker describes another such spiritual awakening through her character, Shug, in the novel *The Color Purple*. Shug has found reason, as a black woman, to reject her earlier ways of thinking about the *Divine*, and to explore other possibilities. She says,

> My first step from the old white man was trees. Then air. Then birds. Then other people. But one day when I was sitting quiet and feeling like a motherless child, which I was, it come to me: that feeling of being part of everything, not separate at all. I knew that if I cut a tree, my arm would bleed. And I laughed and I cried and I run all around the house. I knew just what it was.[45]

Shug says, "I believe God is everything... Everything that is or ever was or ever will be. And when you can feel that, and be happy to feel that, you've found It."[46]

What might enable our perception to burst open like that? Our experience of consciousness is simultaneously familiar and mysterious. Jill Bolte Taylor was a brain scientist who had a debilitating stroke at the age of thirty-seven. A blood vessel burst in the left side of her brain. Because of her training, she was able to observe her own mind deteriorate as she lost the capacity to think, talk, read, write, or recall any of her life. But there was a surprise in this—as her left brain shut down, her right brain took over, and she entered a different form of consciousness. She experienced something like *kensho*; she felt an all-encompassing sense of blissful, timeless unity with the universe.

Years later, after she recovered the skills of the left brain, she wrote the book, *My Stroke of Insight*, to describe her journey and what she learned. She says,

> To the right mind, no time exists other than the present moment, and each moment is vibrant with sensation. Life or death occurs in the present moment. The experience of joy happens in the present moment. Our perception and experience of connection with something that is greater than ourselves occurs in the present

moment. To our right mind, the moment of *now* is timeless and abundant.[47]

During her stroke, Taylor lost the sense of herself as a separate being, yet she gained an experience of herself as the whole universe. Perhaps, the spiritual journey is not so much a journey through time, but a journey out of time, from one form of perception to another. In order to enter this experience of the present moment, which is also the experience of eternity, perhaps we must move from our left-brain awareness to our right-brain awareness.

I am usually a left-brain sort of person. I like the way the left brain organizes everything and notices patterns. It tells a story from the memories of my life, and tries to make meaning and find the purpose of things. I appreciate how it can see the patterns of the planets and stars and moon, and create calendars. I like to listen and read and write and talk. One of my spiritual practices has been to journal, and I can see this is a very left-brain spiritual practice, a way to tell a story and make meaning about my life.

My own experience of the *Divine* has usually been somewhat like a conversation, an encounter involving words, talking or listening. It is a stretch for me to imagine a being-less, word-less unity. In order to find the right-brain awareness, I must quiet the chatter of the left brain.

The right brain has the capacity to appreciate the miracle of life right now: that I am here, that my cells work together to see and hear and taste and touch. The right brain has the capacity to experience the connection between myself and the larger whole of which I am a part. The right brain is inherently grateful and nonjudgmental, compassionate and curious, awake to beauty and joy. The right brain is aware of the dance of life, not attached to a separated small being, but joined to a flow of energy not divisible by time or space.

I feel this awareness in fleeting ways, in brief moments. I feel it when the earth is waking up in the springtime. I feel it when I see the stars on a dark night. I feel it when I float on the salt water of the ocean. I imagine I will recognize it if suddenly I lose myself in the unity of it all.

However, when I take seriously this interconnected web of all being, I also come face to face with my own attachment to separation. I sense what it asks is more than a mystical appreciation of the beauty of the larger whole. There is also a kind of terror within it. Something within me, and perhaps within many of us, is afraid of letting down the walls and opening the heart. I am afraid of feeling the pain of other people, I am afraid of feeling the pain of the earth. I am afraid of letting go of my illusion of control, I am afraid of being hurt by other people, or emptied out by other people.

If I want to experience the larger whole, the path will be through my own consciousness, my own mind and heart. So I have to confront what is in my heart—its brokenness as well as its beauty. The first step toward experiencing inner wholeness is to acknowledge our brokenness. I observed this many times during my practice as a psychotherapist. As painful events happen in our lives, we learn to block off the memories and feelings that cause our pain. We become divided from ourselves, and divided from others. I notice how we may shut down the anger we feel, or despise the needy child deep within us. The first step in healing is to acknowledge those parts of ourselves we have broken off.

As a therapist, I used the healing processes of psychodrama. We would begin by imagining the broken off parts of the self as separate entities. A woman comes in for therapy, anxious and lonely, and we use an empty chair to represent her loneliness. I invite her to talk to the empty chair as if it were her loneliness. At first she is dismissive and says to the loneliness, "I don't need anything from you. Just stop bothering me." But then I ask her to move over and sit in the chair of the loneliness, to imagine herself being the loneliness talking back to her. In that other chair, tears start to fall, and something like a light dawns in her eyes. The tears bring a kind of healing.

Once she lets herself actually feel the loneliness, she is restored to herself. Her thoughts and feelings become one, and ironically, she feels less alone. She has brought the loneliness back together with her own center.

People often come to therapy thinking they are going to get rid of the pain inside themselves. But they find healing only when they have learned to embrace the brokenness with love. It is that embracing of the pain which finally eases their pain. We have to cultivate an inner coming together of our many parts. If we cannot embrace all the parts of the self, how can we embrace all the parts beyond the self.

When I was a child, I had two names. My mother wanted to name me *Michael*, remembering a girl from her childhood who had that name. She thought it was a beautiful name for a girl. But my dad's mother said, you can't name a girl *Michael*, and the force of her personality resulted in a compromise. The name was written *Michel* on my birth certificate, half way between *Michael* and *Michele*, and I was called *Mike* at home and *Michele* at school.

At home, *Mike* seemed like a totally fine name. But during my frequent school changes, I was always afraid the teacher would pronounce my name *Michael*, instead of *Michele*. At school, it felt strange to have this name that could be a boy's name. And because I was a skinny stick of a child, it wasn't necessarily obvious whether I was a boy or a girl (unless I was wearing a school uniform skirt). I didn't want to be weird when I was trying to fit in to a new place.

When I got to college, I decided to adopt *Michele* as my full-time name. But in my mid-twenties, when I started to study psychodrama, these divided parts of myself came to the surface again. I did a session in which each of my named selves were invited to talk to each other and to the therapist. Michele was the public face I presented to the world, the good girl who did what she was told, and tried to have everything under control. She got good grades, and wanted to fit in. She always appeared calm, and her style was optimistic and romantic.

Michael was more hidden and complex. At home, she had been creative and adventurous, but she was afraid to show her face to the public. She felt her feelings deeply—sadness, loneliness, anger about having to move so often, fear about the financial troubles of her family, and the conflicts they provoked between her parents. She sometimes wanted to rage or cry, but rarely shared those feelings.

And there I was, sitting between these two, trying to mediate. *Michael* was angry at *Michele*, and *Michele* was afraid of *Michael*. In the psychodrama session, I sat in each of those chairs, one after the other. I felt a pain in my stomach. I felt short of breath. I was encouraged to breathe deeply in each place, to breathe into the pain in my stomach.

Gradually I realized I had banished the *Michael* part of me, and tried to become *Michele*. I knew I needed to reclaim the pronunciation *Michael* as a way to bring back those hidden and forgotten parts of me, to return to my original naming, and to stop wearing the mask I had worn. It was scary, and I had to endure endless questions about my unusual name. But it led me on a path of greater integration and authenticity.

Of course, you may notice the current spelling of my name is not *Michel*. After several years of being called *Mike*, I experienced the profound transformation feminism brought into my life. As women working out our own liberation, we were reclaiming words, and respelling words to mark that new identity. We spelled the word *woman* as *womyn*, to mark ourselves as central to ourselves, not secondary to "man." During that time, I also chose that *y* to mark my name—the same pronunciation, but a reminder of the change that transformed everything about my life. And so I became *Myke* or *Mykel*.

I think perhaps many of us come to spirituality hoping to ease the pain within. The name *Michele* was like that for me. Sweetness and light and trying to be optimistic. But real spirituality will pull us into the larger interweaving dance of all life. Brokenness too is a part of that dance. We have to cultivate a welcome to all the broken parts, in order to bring everything together. Pain and joy, birth and death, calm and storm. We must embrace the brokenness of the world to let ourselves experience our *Divine* connection.

We must even embrace the walls we find in our hearts. I had to recognize the divisions that were symbolized by my two names. We have to be aware of our separateness in order to come to awareness of our unity. Because this is how we are. Here I am in this moment, alive and part of the great circle of life. All the feelings I feel, including fear and separation and anger and despair, are part of the universe at this moment. I have learned that, somehow, the task that matters, the only dance I must do, is to pay attention to the present moment, and then the next present moment with its own brokenness and wholeness. I am asked to take one step forward, to make the one next choice toward connection.

What helps me to do this is the breath. When I don't know what to do, I can breathe into my emotions. Breathe into fear, breathe into anger, breathe into loneliness, breathe into the impulse to control. As I practice breathing into the parts within, I am gradually able to breathe also into the parts beyond me. Breathe into the pain of the world, breathe into the beauty of the world, breathe into what I notice and perceive, breathe into what I cannot heal. As I breathe into the parts, they soften and the edges begin to dissolve.

Breathing is the first prayer, and it is the practice of a lifetime. As we breathe, we are interconnected with all breathers of air. As we imagine our breath entering all the broken-off pieces of self and world, we bring everything together, we discover what is already true, that we are always one. The threads of interconnection weave their way into the center of our being, and hold us one to the other.

PRACTICE

When you encounter a feeling
from which you want to run away
or which you want to cast aside,
go toward it instead.
Sit still, and breathe deeply.
Notice where in your body you feel that feeling.
Does it have a shape?
Does it have a color?
Imagine your breath moving from your lungs
to the place in your body where the feeling lives.
Don't try to change or get rid of the feeling, only observe.
Keep breathing.
Imagine what you might like to say to the feeling.
Imagine what the feeling might like to say to you.
Breathe some more.

9: Diving and Floating

I love to go into the water. People who know me laugh about how early in the season I jump into the ocean. Most people in Maine don't venture out except in July and August. I don't do the polar bear swims in the middle of winter. It is not about physical prowess or self-torture or even boldness. But sometimes early in spring, there will be a freakishly hot day, and if the high tide comes in the late afternoon, the water in the bay has been warming up under the sun for a little while. Then I might venture out, briefly, a quick dip as if to say hello, here I am. It's very cold and very exhilarating. It transforms the whole day.

Growing up, I liked to play and swim in the quiet waters of Michigan's small lakes and ponds. We didn't live right next to a lake, so swimming was more an occasional treat than an everyday habit. But it was important to my mom that all of her children learn to swim. This was a result of my mom's early experience of a storm coming up on Pontiac Lake while she was out rowing with her mother. She knew how to swim, but her mother did not; she was afraid her mother would drown and she wouldn't be able to save her. They made it to shore, but she resolved that her children wouldn't face such a danger.

When I was in college, I played in the fresh water waves of the vast Lake Michigan, and watched the sun go down over its endless sparkling blue horizon. It was thrilling to experience the breakers as high as our heads, the force of those strong waters pushing against our small bodies. People are surprised by how much Lake Michigan is like the ocean. But I didn't encounter the salty embrace of the Atlantic until I moved to Boston in my thirties. I still remember the sharpness of its scent, the pleasurable buoyancy of arms and legs, and the utter surprise of its taste on my lips, even though I knew it should be salty. Something about the ocean resonated in the deepest part of me.

One summer day when we were living on Cape Cod, Margy and I went to Nauset Beach with visiting friends, whose twelve-year-old daughter had never been swimming in the ocean. The waves were crashing against the stony beach, and the water was icy to our toes. With appropriate groans and squeals, we pushed through the foamy current to get to a spot we could stand in without falling over.

We were happy to show one more child the exuberant art of jumping up with the waves as they approached, letting the energy of the water lift us and drop us down. Then there was the other option: diving into and under the waves, and resurfacing as they receded. We all laughed and jumped and yielded to the overwhelming force all around us. The ocean didn't swallow us as we played in the waves along the shore, yet we experienced some small part of the immensity of its power.

Going into the water is a spiritual practice for me. This especially became true when I lived on Cape Cod surrounded by water. Within fifteen minutes of our house there were multiple opportunities for going into the water. The cool, sweet quiet of the ponds, surrounded by trees deciduous and evergreen. The pounding waves of the ocean that can knock you down or lift you up. And my favorite, the shining bright waters of the bay, whose golden sand reflects back the rippling sun so it seems as if you are swimming in dancing light.

To enter the water restores my spirit in a visceral way. Truthfully, I don't do a lot of actual swimming. Mostly it is about diving under and floating on the surface. How can I describe it? At first, there is the shock of wading into the biting cold, and I sometimes have to cry out with each step. It creates a kind of thunderstorm in my body chemistry—perhaps it is the adrenaline? It wakes me up from wherever I have been and thankfully switches on an inner thermostat: my body fires up its own sources of heat.

Once I reach the depth where the water is up to my chest, I dive under a few times, so the very top of my head feels the cold, while my eyes open in the pale green and cloudy swirling of the underworld. Then I surface again, lean back and let myself float. Another transformation begins. As the water holds me up, my own weight seems to decrease—and whatever heaviness I feel also decreases. The water holds up all the burdens of my body and heart. When there are somewhat larger waves, I don't float on my back, so much as gently tread water, like floating sitting up, with the water up to my chest or shoulders. I alternate standing and letting my feet drift upward from the sand.

The water rocks my body in a gentle rhythm and the movements of the waves are like a thousand little massages on my skin. I feel like I am being danced from the outside in. I am like a baby being rocked in the arms of a mother. The sounds are soothing, and the salt on my skin is invisibly shifting the ions in my body. The elements are all coming together—the water surrounding my body and the air on my face, the earth as sand under my feet and the fire of the sun warm on my face and igniting the water with radiance.

This floating, this being held again, enables me to enter the realm of absolute trust and surrender. In the water I can let go of anxiety, fear, anger, sadness. I can let go of any of the burdens that weigh me down. I can let go of the illusion that I am in control. As the ocean supports and rocks my physical being, my emotional and spiritual being feel lighter, comforted, restored. There are so many griefs we carry as human beings, so many worries, and all of it can feel so much bigger than we are. But the ocean is bigger than any of my troubles.

What does it mean to give myself over to this great power? What does it mean to be held by this great power? I am reminded of the idea of a sacrament I learned as a child. A sacrament is an outward symbol of an inward mystery. For me, all waters—lakes and streams and rivers, but especially the ocean— are a symbol and manifestation of the great *Mystery*, the larger whole, the *Divine*.

The water reveals to me that divinity is deeper and wider and wiser than I can imagine, that I can trust the unfolding of my life within the larger Life of the universe. I can give myself into this larger flow, this larger *Energy*. Spirituality is a kind of diving and floating in the larger *Energy*—taking a risk that if we let go, if we surrender to the *Mystery*, it will embrace us and hold us up. We can move beyond the small boundaries of self into the unity of the whole, into beauty, love, interconnection. We are bodily creatures, and when our bodies can surrender, our spirits can also surrender. When I float in the water, my mind can let go, and enter into being, into the present moment, into *Mystery*.

Coming out of the water is then like being born anew. Perhaps we feel this because our bodies remember. We were born out of the salt waters of our mother's womb. In the deep dawn of history, our species ancestors also emerged from the sea. We swaddle ourselves in towels and lay down on a warm bed of sand. We return to everyday life refreshed, and we sleep like babies when night comes.

I have known moments of deep unity floating in the ocean. But I have to admit I am still very much a landlubber in my relationship to the sea; I am only beginning to explore its mysteries. To surrender, to move beyond and outside of the self, can be disorienting and uncomfortable. I am reminded of the first time I went on a whale watch, many years ago now. The surface of the sea was rough, and I got very sick. My dignity was partially redeemed by the fact that members of the whale watch crew were also sick that day. We never saw any whales. I spent the three hours curled up on a bench inside, vomiting into a plastic bag. When we came back to the dock in Provincetown, I stepped ashore with great relief.

But surprisingly, I also felt another feeling: a sense of having been through some sacred initiation. The power of the ocean had taken over my body, and I was a small animal held in its arms, with no choice but to yield to the experience. Perhaps it may seem strange to celebrate a powerful bout of seasickness. But it felt like another layer of surrender to the deep. It felt like another layer of understanding. The ocean, like the *Spirit*, is larger than ourselves, beautiful and generous, but also dangerous and unpredictable. We are drawn to it, yet challenged by it, washed by it, and sometimes turned upside down by it.

Shortly after Margy and I moved to Cape Cod, the movie *The Perfect Storm* was showing at area theaters. It is a story of six men who lost their lives when their sword fishing boat, the Andrea Gail, disappeared in the hundred foot waves of the Halloween storm of 1991. It reminded me of the dangerous side of the ocean, the unpredictability and power of its storms. So many people over many centuries have lost their lives upon the sea. It is fierce and can be devastating.

And yet sailors and fishermen venture into the vastness of that danger every day. In her book *The Hungry Ocean*, Linda Greenlaw acknowledges the love-hate dynamic that sailors can feel when setting out on a fishing trip.[48] How easy it would be to drop out, to stay on shore. There is relief that comes when they are too far out to swim back to shore. The work of the crew, even in good weather, is back-breaking, exhausting, dangerous, and a gamble.

But fishermen return again and again, to work twenty-hour stretches for days, through rain and storm, to bring in a full hold of fish and a paycheck, if they are lucky. Greenlaw observes "the most miserable people are those who fish out of necessity rather than out of a love of the sea…"[49] For her and others like her, there is a thrill in catching fish, a deep satisfaction in going to sea and returning to shore.

When I think back on the journey of my relationship with *Mystery*, I am reminded of those years when everything I thought I knew was washed away. I had to leave behind the familiar rituals of my Catholic youth; an awareness of the oppression of women took away the comforting images of the *divine Father* who I thought would always hold me in His arms. All of that was swept away in a tsunami of awakening before a strange *divinity* without gender or race or face or dogma. There were times I felt like I was drowning in confusion and loneliness and grief. Yet I was always carried and I was always called further out. I was held up, washed, and birthed anew.

Chickasaw writer Linda Hogan says, of those many who have gone to sea through the years,

> The sea is a primal magnet, and maybe theirs were journeys into mystery and wilderness, a pull toward healing, toward a baptism in

the enormous world of life, a coming together of land creatures with the holy waters of earth that carry not only ships and giant fish, but also our own hidden treasures.[50]

Many religious traditions have rituals involving immersion in water. In the Jewish tradition, *God* was present in the waters of the Red Sea, to divide the sea and make a way for the Israelite people to escape from slavery. Their passage to freedom was through the waters. Later, they entered the Promised Land through the River Jordan. The ongoing ritual bath of the *Mikveh* invites Jews to be purified by immersion in living waters. The ministry of Jesus began in his baptism in the River Jordan, and the ritual of baptism has endured over two thousand years as the major ceremony of Christian initiation.

A spiritual leader from Zimbabwe, Mandaza Kandemwa, visited my congregation when I was on Cape Cod, and spoke to us about the water ceremonies they practice in Zimbabwe. In the Shona language, the water spirits are called *njuzu*. These spirits are focused on healing and peacemaking. In their rituals a person was submerged four times in the waters of a river or stream. Those who were called to be healers were also initiated by submersion in the waters of the river.

As I learned about and reflected on the water ceremonies that have been a part of so many traditions, I was inspired to bring more ceremony into my own going into the water. I created a ritual of diving under the water four times, facing each of the four directions, north, east, south and west. Each time, as I dove under, I would let go of any burdens or attachments I was holding, plans for the future or things left undone in the past. In each direction, I would focus on particular attachments that seemed related to that direction. Most of all, I would let go of my illusions of control. I would give thanks for the blessings in my life. Then I would float on my back, and let the water hold me up, and let the *Divine Mystery* carry me.

I began to go into the water almost every day. Going into salt water is a powerful kind of communion with the large ocean, but for this daily practice, I was drawn to the fresh water ponds. Each has its own kind of energy. Ponds are gentle and refreshing, and not quite so cold. One year, starting in April, each morning I would drive ten minutes over to Cliff Pond, dive four times into the water and float there for ten minutes, and then drive home. I kept going in the summer, and into the fall, when the water stayed surprisingly warm.

I created a song to sing as a prayer. The repeating refrain goes like this:

Water we thank you, for washing clear our burdens.
Water we thank you, for bringing growth to seedlings.
Let the water heal you, let the water hold you,
Let the water fill you, all is one.

I give thanks every day I live only a short drive away from holy waters. Of course, the waters of my current home in Maine are not the same as the waters of Cape Cod. There are more rocky shores and less golden sand. The water is colder here. When I moved to Maine, I could no longer go into the water every day. The nearest ponds were at least thirty or forty minutes away from our house. Not so easy for short daily rituals. The closest water was twenty minutes away. It was a tidal beach, one of many small coves and inlets that drain out with the low tide, and fill up with the high tide. So we could only swim there for two hours before or after the high tide. Still, there was something I loved about that, because it required us to pay attention to the tides. Each day the high tides are about fifty minutes later than the day before. It kept me in tune with the cyclic rhythms of the sea and the moon.

Diving under the water has to be a more occasional ceremony now. I grieved that loss deeply when we moved from Cape Cod. But here I am surrounded by tall trees again, and so that helps me to adapt. When we open our spirits to connecting to the natural world, we discover each place has its own rituals and blessings. Each season has its own gifts. To create a spiritual practice with the natural world is to develop a relationship to a particular place and season. Just like each person is unique and each human relationship is unique. There are no substitutions. A lake is not the sea. A forest is not the beach. A desert is not the mountain. Each place has its gifts.

But water is everywhere human beings are. Perhaps in some places we cannot dive into water or float in it. Perhaps in some places water is scarce and difficult to access. But each time we bathe in water, we can enter it with mindfulness. Each time we feel the rain, we can pause for a moment before we run for cover, let it bless us. This *Mystery* is all around us, it is deep within us.

PRACTICE

If you live near a body of water, go into it.
Imagine letting go of your burdens
as you dive underneath the surface
Dive under as often as you need to,
until you aren't carrying anything anymore.
Then float on the surface of the water,
and let yourself imagine you are floating in the Divine.
Give thanks.
Feel free to make up your own tune to my water ritual song.
You can also do this in a pool,
if that is what you have access to.
You can do it in the bath or shower,
letting the water wash away your burdens.

10: The Power We Hold

My love for the earth, the cardinals, the trees, and the ocean inspires me to take action to change the way we human beings live, so that we stop destroying these beings and our own habitat. It inspires me to join in protests, in political lobbying, in civil disobedience against such destruction. Poet activist Audre Lorde advises, "Use what power you have to work for what you believe in."[51]

As I tap into my connection to the larger *Mystery*, as I surrender myself to be a part of its energetic flow, I also gain access to a spiritual energy that can shape, create, and cause change and healing throughout the whole. In my life, this spiritual energy has been called *prayer* or *magic*, depending on the context in which it was exercised. One context was in my youth as a Catholic Pentecostal. We prayed by laying our hands on the person for whom we prayed. The other context was in circles of women who were re-inventing ourselves as feminist witches. We were more likely to do rituals, to light candles, to visualize what we desired. Pentecostals called it *prayer*, witches called it *magic*, but it was the same process.

When we face a challenge that feels bigger than we are, we can consciously join our small energies to the larger energies of the universe. We can appeal to the earth and the moon, and the trees and the ancestors, we can appeal to the *Divine* forces of kindness and harmony, to aid us in our vision and in our vulnerability. Right in the midst of our limitations, even in our utter helplessness, we can discover limitless energies beyond our own personal effort.

As children, each of us needed the help of someone larger than us. We relied on our parents or other caregivers for everything—our food, our shelter, our learning, our basic needs. That may have been a nurturing experience or a painful one. As we grow up in our culture, we feel a pull to become independent, to be able to do things for ourselves. As adults, we are working to find a balance between giving and receiving, between helping others and getting help when we need it. But for many of us asking for help is difficult. Probably because we don't like to experience our vulnerability, our smallness. Possibly because we've had the experience of asking for help and not receiving it, or being taken advantage of when we were in need. So there might be emotional baggage attached to the idea of prayer or magic.

And how many of us have known the anguish of an unanswered prayer? When I was in college I fell in love with a classmate, and fervently begged *God* to let him fall in love with me too. But it never happened. Another time, an old man told me that as a small boy he had prayed to *God* to heal his mother when she was dying. It broke his heart when she did not get well, and he never prayed again. When I think about prayer I remember that anguish. And yet, for me, there are also other memories. There have been times when, to my astonishment, strange and wonderful things happened after prayer. As if, despite making an appeal, I never really expected a response.

Several years ago, my youngest brother in Michigan was getting married. My family members are scattered across the country, and it is rare for us to be able to gather all together. At that time, our finances were very tight, but I hoped Margy and I could attend the wedding, since she hadn't had a chance to meet most of my family yet. We found out two tickets would cost $850. We couldn't afford that. So I prayed for a way to get to the wedding; and I also called my Pentecostal mystic dad and asked him to pray. And no, he did not send us the tickets. However, the very next morning, an email came announcing special bargain fares from a certain airline. The two of us could go for a total cost of $325.

Can prayer or magic work? I believe it works when some sort of transformation happens. Sometimes, the transformation is within us—we grow, our hearts heal, we deepen our connection to the larger *Mystery*, we feel a deep peace in that connection. We feel seen and understood.

In the mid-1980s I joined with other women at the Seneca Women's Encampment for a Future of Peace and Justice. Called the Women's Peace Camp, for short, it was set up to protest nuclear weapons at the Seneca Army Depot in upstate New York. Organizers had purchased a fifty-two-acre farm that bordered the Depot, and started a campground for activists from around the world to join in ongoing non-violent protests against the Depot. We offered educational workshops, did publicity concerning nuclear weapons, and held vigils at the gate to the Depot, which was just down the road.

We also created a magic circle on the land where we would do rituals, and sing and dance and pray for peace. The magic of the Women's Peace Camp did not shut down the Seneca Army Depot while we were there. (It was closed years later.) But it did transform our lives, including mine. I felt a new sense of purpose. I gained strength to live my values. I made lasting connections with these women and with the earth. Our vision for the future was made manifest in a tangible way, and I could never forget it. It is much harder to measure the effects of our magic on the shifting of the larger world. Perhaps we will never know what it added to the cause of peace.

But prayer or magic can also create transformation on a very practical level, especially for specific identified concerns. During the spring of 1986, there were only a few of us at the Camp, staying in the old farmhouse that was on the land. My prayer that evening was not for world peace. At that time, my lover was living in western Massachusetts, and I missed her. I didn't have a car, or much money. My prayer was a wish I might find a way to go visit her.

The camp was a crossroads of sorts, and it wasn't uncommon for us to have visitors. Peace activists from all over would stop in for a day or a week. Not so many during the winter or spring, but still a few. In my prayer, I was conscious of my wish to see my love, and I imagined someone coming like a knight on a white horse to carry me to Massachusetts.

The very next day someone pulled into the driveway. The visitor was driving to Massachusetts in a white pickup truck. It would have been enough to get a ride, which I did. But the white pickup truck was an added synchronistic touch that still sends goose bumps up my arms. So whimsical and tender a response.

What causes our prayer to work, or not to work? Larry Dossey is a physician who attempted to study prayer scientifically. He challenges the way we have been taught to think about prayer and *God*. He says people think of sending prayers "upward," as if *God* were a spiritual communications satellite, granting or denying requests at whim. He feels the studies seem to point, not to the arbitrary power of that kind of *God*, but to some inherent power within the human being, something linking us together beyond the limits of space and time.[52]

When we open up a connection to the larger whole, our energy—the latent divinity or *Mystery Seed* within us—tunes in to larger energies. We can be influenced by those energies, and also influence the energy of that whole, in subtle and significant ways. Prayer and magic, then, are a particular kind of paying attention, a doorway, a linkage, based on recognizing the relationship between our individual self and the other energies of the universe.

So I believe we can learn how to pray, how to better activate that linkage. As I have mentioned before, the tool of imagination is important in working with intangible energies. For example, I sometimes think of the energies like a flow of water. If we dive into and relax in a large body of water, we can float; we can also choose to draw water into our bodies by drinking it, we can shape water, use it to cause change, create something with it. Prayer and magic are like that. We connect to the larger reality through opening up or diving in, and then we direct that water toward a need or a hope.

Both Catholic Pentecostals and feminist witches have a view of prayer or magic that gives great importance to the power within us, rather than an appeal for far away help. The Pentecostals call it the *Holy Spirit* working through us. The witches' circles invoke the *Goddess*, the feminine *Divine*, who is within all things, an energy which our own hands can shape and direct to our intentions. Because of these communities, I had the chance to observe, practice, and experiment with prayer and magic, and feel their possibilities for my life. When I look back at my experience, I see there are certain qualities that contribute to prayers with tangible results.

First we need to become aware of the desires and yearnings in our hearts. I would even say that desire or yearning, or felt need, is the key to the power in prayer, the way to unlock its energy. It may take a great deal of introspection to know what we truly desire, or it may lie hidden in plain sight like a throw-away wish.

Some of us have learned to pay so much attention to the needs and desires of others that we don't know how to get in touch with our own. Or we may have been misled by advertising, which manipulates our desires toward the pursuit of consumer products. Some of us may feel we don't deserve what we desire. At times in my life, I felt my religion asked me to give up my own desires. But now I believe our deep desires come from a sacred place. We are all sacred beings and worthy of receiving good from this world. In prayer, we must welcome our true desire, our yearning, our tender wishes.

And then, we need to send that yearning or that desire out into the universe. I often imagine it like shooting an arrow from a bow. A big part of shooting an arrow is letting it go. Letting go of our desire does not mean abandoning it, or giving up on it. Letting go means not clinging to the need. An arrow can't reach its mark if we hang on to it. We must trust that if we send out the arrow, it will have an effect. Prayer is not the same thing as worry. Worry is a kind of hanging on, imagining the worst future, rather than being open to the possibility of something good. So we send it out and let go.

All desire, all magic, has a risk attached to it. If we let ourselves feel desire, we risk the pain of it not being fulfilled. That became easier for me when I understood that our desire is holy whether it is fulfilled or not. Desire is only unholy if it harms other people or disregards their freedom. We must hold a deep respect for all beings. Prayer and magic are not coercive. For example, if I am romantically attracted to someone, I can honor that desire as holy. But I can't force the other person to be attracted back. Letting go of the arrow honors the powers beyond us, as well as the powers within us. We are joining forces with the universe, not trying to force the universe to do our bidding.

Sending out the arrow is a symbol of asking for help, of joining our energy to the larger reality. Here again, the arrow is only one image. There might be other images that work better to make it real for us. We might imagine planting our desire like a seed in the fertile soil. We might imagine it like one small channel of a stream entering into a great river of life. We can also send forth our prayers into the care of our friends. We can tell other people what we desire and need. When we join our power with the power of others, it grows stronger.

We also need to take some action on our own behalf. This includes both mental action and physical action. Mental action is whatever we do that uses the tool of imagination I have been speaking about. Several years ago, when I lived on Cape Cod, a Wampanoag grandmother gave me a trouble basket. She said, "Whenever you are worrying about something or feeling sad, you can put that trouble in the basket. You can write it on a piece of paper, or hold a stone, and imagine your trouble in the stone, and then put it in the basket, close the lid, and let go. It won't feel so heavy."

Images focus and shape the energy generated by our desire, so we can work with it. The image of the stone in the basket can focus our letting go of trouble. Or for another example, if we desire to heal someone we love, we may imagine a rainbow light flowing through their body. The image of rainbow light gives a form to our desire for their healing. We can also use material objects to focus our imagination. When we light a candle, the light of healing becomes more tangible. The more vivid the image, the more powerful the energy can be.

We take action in our imagination, but we also need to take action in our daily life, to bring our desire into being. Prayer and magic are not a substitute for action in the world; rather they go hand in hand. If we want to find a place to live, usually we must go out looking for one. Years ago, four of my friends and I wanted to rent a big house in Jamaica Plain so we could live as a community. We lit a candle with our desire, and then we went out and looked at all the houses advertised in the paper. But nothing seemed right all day, so we finally stopped for ice cream. Next to our booth was a bulletin board, and there we found a new poster for a house to rent. We called and it turned out to be our perfect house, three doors away from the ice cream parlor.

When we commit ourselves to a course of action, the universe responds. It is not a formula, it is an invitation. I find the universe often responds in ways we don't quite expect. We didn't find our house in the paper where we looked. We found it right after we stopped looking. The universe seems to have a sense of the ironic. Why else would the ride to see my love in Massachusetts have arrived in the form of a white pickup truck? There has often been synchronicity and humor in my own experience with prayer or magic.

But what if it doesn't seem to work? What if our desire is not fulfilled? Here is what I have found in my life. Occasionally, not always, something is awry inside my own heart. Maybe I haven't really discovered my deepest desire, and prayer helps me to find my true center. Maybe I discover I was afraid to take action on my own behalf. By opening our hearts to the movement of desire, of risk, of action, we release great energy. In this way, the work of prayer fosters transformation within us that may go beyond our initial desire.

But sometimes, if our prayer is not fulfilled, it is just that there is no match out there corresponding to our desire. There was another time when I was praying for housing in Jamaica Plain, and it took four months before I found something. During those months, I'd often imagine a particular solution, and something amazing would show up, but then it wouldn't be quite right. I remember one day I did an errand on St. John's Road, and thought, this would be a nice street to live on. Then later that day, a person came into the bookstore where I worked, and told me about an apartment there. I followed the lead with excitement, but found out it was too expensive.

Four months went by with such near misses and close calls. I wondered sometimes if the universe was playing games with my hopes and needs, but eventually I decided to blame a tough housing market. Prayers can't work to find housing for all who need it, without our taking some collective action to create more affordable housing. People shouldn't have to work magic to find a place to live.

Sometimes, when we release our desire into the universe, the answer comes in ways we didn't realize we wanted. I think about my last year at my previous congregation. I had been the Associate Minister there for several years, and then the Senior Minister decided to move on to a new post. When that happens, it is extremely rare that an Associate Minister can remain, or be promoted to the Senior Ministry position. But what I felt in my heart at that time was a deep desire to stay on Cape Cod, and grow my ministry there. So I pursued that possibility, and prayed for that possibility, even as I did the necessary preparation to explore other options.

It didn't work out for me to stay, and I felt sad about it, but then I was chosen to be the Minister of my current congregation in Maine. Very quickly, I realized this was the best place for me to be. But I also believe my choice to pursue the desire of my heart as I understood it, created in me the strength that enabled me to be chosen for a new ministry. I sent that arrow into the universe, and it landed in exactly the right place, even though it was a different place from where I had aimed it. It felt like my prayer was answered.

Poet Elizabeth Cunningham says, "You can only pray what's in your heart." We can only pray our desire, our suffering, our hunger, our turmoil, our joy. She says, "pray your heart into the great quiet hands that can hold it/ like the small bird it is."[53]

In the end, prayer and magic return us to the transformation of being held and heard by the larger energies in the web. The best listener is not the person who tries to solve our problems or fix our dilemmas. The best listener is the one who cherishes us exactly the way we are. Who lets us talk and feel and sort something out by being present to us in compassion. So it is with the best prayer or magic as well. We open our hearts, and we feel heard, we feel held, we feel cherished by this great quiet *Kindness*.

PRACTICE

Reflect on the needs and desires of your heart.
Choose one small desire that is important to you.
Imagine sending that desire out into the universe
like an arrow, or in whatever image fits it best.

Take one action on your own behalf
that is directed to your desire.
Then, let it go.
Don't be attached to any outcome.
Pay attention to how the universe
might be responding to your prayer.
Watch for transformation of some kind.
Give thanks.
May the Kindness above you
and the Kindness below you,
and the Kindness waiting in every direction
bless you and help you on your journey.

11: All the Water Is One Water

One summer several years ago, I attended a two-week Earth Activist Training, which combined a Permaculture Design Course with practice in magical and political work on behalf of the earth. We began with a water ritual. We brought water from the places we lived or the places we may have traveled to pour into one container. At the end, each person took some of the water, and we brought it home with us. One of the teachers for the training was feminist witch and eco-activist Starhawk, whose writings had been important for me earlier in my spiritual journey. She had begun collecting water in this way many years ago. She brought water back from her travels around the world, and asked her friends to bring back water when they went to far off places. They brought water from the sacred Ganges River in India, and from the great Nile River in Egypt; they even brought melted ice from Antarctica. After a while, they had water from every continent.

When you pour it into one container, all of the water mixes together, and every drop has some of the molecules of water from every place. So if you take a small bottle of water out, you have the waters from many places in one bottle. Each time you have a water ritual, you add some water from the bottle you saved from the previous ritual. In that way, each ritual, each small bottle, contain the waters from all over the world.

Why would we want to have a small bottle of waters from everywhere in the world? For me, first of all, it is one more way to make tangible the sacredness of water. All life comes from water, and needs water to survive. Water moves through the whole ecosystem, nurturing and transforming life as it moves. It rises from the ocean in evaporation, forming clouds in the sky, and, blown by the winds, it returns to the land in the form of rain or snow. This precipitation falls into the soil, and gathers in streams and aquifers. In the midst of this journey, it also travels through the bodies of every living thing.

Margy and I have a bird bath outside our back door. Many kinds of birds come to drink the water we keep filled there, but we've also seen squirrels, chipmunks, and bees stop to drink. Every being needs water: insects, birds, mammals, fish, humans. Water also rises up into the stems of plants and the trunks of trees. But none of the water is isolated from the rest—even our own bodies are part of the watershed. We drink in the water, it moves through our blood, and permeates all of our cells, and then we sweat it out or pee it out. Sometimes we weep with wet salty tears. The water goes back to the air or the earth and continues in streams and rivers on its way to the ocean. The cycle keeps going round and round.

All the water on earth is really one water, continuously flowing through the biosphere. Even if we get water from our kitchen tap, that water has been around the world on its journey. All water is connected, and connects all of life.

My little bottle of the waters of the world also reminds me that we need not only ritual, but also practical action to take care of water. When I was ten, my family went on vacation to the mountains of Wyoming. I remember coming upon a stream that had a little sign saying Potable Water. My sisters and I were very excited we could drink right out of the stream. The water tasted funny to us, with its enhanced mineral content, but it was cool and refreshing nonetheless. Now, looking back on that event, I am saddened by our amazement at drinking water directly from the earth. For millennia, all people drank from rivers and streams, and animals still do. But in the memories of most of us, this no longer is a part of our expectations about water. We take for granted that pollution has made most water undrinkable unless it is purified.

It may seem as if there is an endless supply of water on the earth. But of all the water on the earth, only one percent is fresh water. More and more water is being polluted, or being diverted to industrial or agricultural use. We have now reached the stage where there is a global crisis looming as drinkable water becomes increasingly scarce.

Oren Lyons, Faithkeeper of the Turtle Clan of the Onandaga Nation, has said, "Keeping the water pure is one of the first laws of life. If you destroy the water, you destroy life. That's what I mean about common sense. Anybody can see that. All life on Mother Earth depends on the pure water, yet we spill every kind of dirt and filth and poison into it."[54]

Analysts are predicting water will be the number-one political issue in the coming years. Just as wars are being fought over oil, so increasingly there are conflicts over access to water. The business solution is to privatize the water: sell it to corporations and let them sell it to the people. The theory is that if water is a scarce resource, then the market should determine its price, and price will regulate its use. But citizens' groups are fighting back to say water cannot be commodified, because it is an absolute necessity for life. We cannot take water out of its relationship to all living beings, and leave it in the hands of a system which is designed to think only in terms of profit.

In Cochabamba, Bolivia, citizens passed a resolution in 2000 to declare:

> 1. Water belongs to the earth and all species and is sacred to life, therefore, the world's water must be conserved, reclaimed and protected for all future generations and its natural patterns respected.
>
> 2. Water is a fundamental human right and a public trust to be guarded by all levels of government, therefore, it should not be commodified, privatized or traded for commercial purposes. These rights must be enshrined at all levels of government. In particular, an international treaty must ensure these principles are noncontrovertable.[55]

In 2010, due to grassroots organizing and lobbying efforts by an international coalition led by Bolivia, the United Nations General Assembly voted overwhelmingly to affirm "the right to safe and clean drinking water and sanitation as a human right that is essential for the full enjoyment of life and all human rights."[56] That doesn't end the battle over commodification, but it becomes one more tool in the struggle to care for the water and ensure its protection.

At the Earth Activist Training we learned about *Permaculture*, a science of designing systems that can meet human needs while regenerating the land around us. Its ethical mandates are to care for the earth, to care for the people, and to share the surplus. I especially loved the cheerful atmosphere of hope and creativity that was engendered. Much of the environmental situation is foreboding and terrifying. But at the training I discovered a merry band of folks who sang while they gardened and went around the world demonstrating alternatives that make a real difference.

Permaculture observes natural patterns to create highly productive environments. For example, it uses the model of the forest to create food forests—gardens of fruit and nut trees, vines, bushes, and ground cover that can function together to feed a family while nurturing the land in a sustainable way. Agribusiness narrowly regards one crop as the only valuable entity, and sees all other life forms as weeds or pests. But if we look more closely at the natural world, we discover diversity is the norm and there are beneficial relationships throughout the plant and animal realms. In one example recounted by bio-chemist Linda Jean Shepherd,

> Researchers at the University of California at Santa Cruz studied the traditional Mexican farming practice of pruning back, rather than pulling, a weed that commonly sprouts between rows of corn. They found that the roots of the weed *Bidens pilosa* secrete compounds lethal to fungi and nematodes that destroy corn. Instead of competing with the corn, the weed controls the pests without significantly stealing soil nutrients from the corn. The practice protects the soil and provides more wholesome food.[57]

The more we learn about nature, the more we see that everywhere diverse plants and animals are interconnected with each other, offering mutual benefit and function; modern agribusiness has ignored this to our detriment. To live sustainably, we must learn from nature, we must open our eyes to the lessons it can teach us about how all beings are related to one another.

Permaculture design also offers sustaining and restorative approaches to our use of water. In a natural landscape, water is absorbed and held in place by plants and trees, and advances very slowly through the ecosystem. When the surface of the earth is covered with concrete for buildings and roads, the water rushes quickly over the surface, picking up pollutants it brings to rivers and lakes. When forests are cut down, or grasslands uprooted for agriculture, the drylands can devolve into desert. Permaculture designers have created tools to slow the water down, and capture it for use. These designs can purify water moving through a system, or reverse the process of desertification.

We learned about and built one such tool, called a *swale*. This is a small ditch created in alignment with the contour of the sloping soil, so rain washing over the soil will be captured, and can be used in plantings near the edge of the swale. The plantings then serve to keep the moisture in the landscape. A swale can also be used to direct water from one area to another. The goal is to slow the flow of water for as long as possible, and thus restore the fertility of the soil, rather than letting the water wash away into creeks that flow rapidly out to rivers and to the sea.

Adopting another practice, Margy and I purchased two rain barrels to collect the rain-water that ran off our garage roof, for use in watering the blueberry bushes and vegetables and flowers we had planted in our front yard. We learned about how high off the ground the barrels needed to be, in order for gravity to pull the water all the way to the plants. We learned that water in a rain barrel heats up in the hot summer sun. We learned how quickly a rainstorm can fill two fifty-gallon barrels.

It is important to take these small steps toward changing our relationship to water use, even in our comparatively water abundant climate in Maine. Even here we need to learn about conserving water and treating it with respect. We face challenges from multinational corporations who bottle our Maine water for sale around the world. The bottled water industry isn't concerned about the water needs of local communities or ecosystems. They negotiate contracts to extract the water for almost nothing, and put it into plastics that end up in the waste system causing further pollution.

Permaculture design follows the principle that in nature there is no waste. What one system doesn't need, another system uses. Our human society wastes an incredible amount of water, even though we know it is scarce. We use it for washing and showering and then let it drain into the septic system or sewer. Why not build gray water systems that take the water from washing and showering and pipe it out for use in the garden?

Some Indigenous stories of North America say we are like a younger sibling on this earth. The other beings and species are more acclimated to their purpose and their relationship to the whole. And so, when we are feeling overwhelmed by the ecological messes we have created, we might turn to our older relatives on the earth to find wisdom for our journey. Permaculture follows this practice by using the wisdom developed by millions of years of evolution, to find solutions for the problems we are facing today.

Water is such a teacher. According to my friend, gkisedtanamoogk, the Wampanoag people consider water a *Manito*, a mysterious life force that has its own life. His people know fresh water as *Nipinapizek*, and regard her as a grandmother. He wrote to me, "i think that we humans only exist because there is a significant number of people who remember to *Give Thanks* to all Those Ones who are the Keepers of Life, one of Those being, *NIPINAPIZEK*. May we continue to Give Thanks...."[58]

When I was growing up Catholic, we used to bless ourselves by touching our fingers in holy water. I associated it with purifying ourselves because we were in some way unclean. But now, the blessing of water feels more like remembering our heritage. We come from water. All water is holy, and we are holy too. We are washed by water, we are restored by water, we are nourished by water.

Each of us faces a choice. Will we approach water as a commodity to be bought and sold, or as a blessing, a teacher to be honored and protected? Water is the mother of all life. There is no life without water. Whether we view it scientifically or spiritually, water is the womb from which all living beings have been born. We are made of water and we need the constant flowing through of water to remain alive in this world. Thankfulness can be the beginning of restoring our relationship with water. If I can remember to be thankful to water, then I have the capacity to take action on its behalf as well. I can join with the many other people who are working for water as a human right, or who work to restore the flow of rivers or clean up pollution in the sea.

The path forward will not be a straight line. I find hope in that. A river or stream meanders on its way to the sea. Because of the friction of the river bed, the water on the bottom of the river moves more slowly than the water on the top. So it creates a spiraling current that wears down one bank and deposits sediment on the other, and then vice versa, as it moves around and around in sweeping curves.[59] Just so, our journey into a new relationship with all life on earth will meander—I imagine in this case, there is more movement at the bottom of our culture, while the top is going much slower. But since we are all connected, movement in any segment has a ripple effect on the whole.

We must keep taking steps, even small steps, in the direction of living in balance with the rest of our interdependent web. We must work our magic and offer thanks and take action in practical and political ways. We must meander in the direction of wholeness, of earth community. Each creative step forward will ripple out into a spiral momentum toward greater balance.

PRACTICE
When I made the conscious choice
to regard water as a blessing,
I decided to stop using plastic bottled water
as much as possible.
I like to carry water with me, so now I carry tap water
in a special reusable metal or glass bottle.
Anytime I drink water,
I am reminded to offer thanks for the blessing.
I invite you to give up plastic bottled water,
and to start carrying water in a reusable container.
Each time you fill or drink from the container,
give thanks to Water for giving us life.

12: Embracing the Broken

Jon Young is the founder of the Wilderness Awareness School in Washington state, which teaches young people skills such as wildlife tracking and plant identification to foster an ecological connection to nature. Many lessons and techniques are easy to learn, and there is a deepening sense of wonder and gratitude that grows along with their skills. But when the youth reach a certain stage in their learning, they hit what he "calls the 'wall of grief,' an experience of being overwhelmed with sorrow at the loss and degradation of the natural world around us."[60] That grief is the most difficult challenge the young people face in all of the school's programs.

I felt such a wall of grief, during the spring and summer of 2010 watching millions of gallons of oil pouring into the Gulf of Mexico from the broken BP deep sea oil well. It seemed as if the earth itself was bleeding from this gaping human-made wound deep below the waters of the sea.

I believe our human survival depends on waking up to our connection to the interdependent web of all existence of which we are a part. The natural world is utterly vital to our lives. The earth is my Bible, my sacred revelation, and my paradise. But that beautiful connection also gives rise to deep sorrow and anguish. We see the melting of ancient glaciers, as the climate heats up from greenhouse gases. We know the topsoil in which our food grows is being depleted, and the rain forests that renew the world's oxygen are being cut down. We know increasing numbers of species are threatened with extinction. We know nuclear stockpiles could destroy most life on earth many times over. We know so much, but we don't know the solutions to these problems that threaten our future. And that, too, is a wall of grief that can stop us in our tracks as we seek to restore our relationship to this earth.

When we affirm a vision of living in harmony with the earth and other beings, we enter an in-between place: we become increasingly aware of the brokenness of our world, but don't yet have access, as individuals, to solutions that fit with our vision. Our entire social and economic system has been built upon the exploitation of the earth for resources, and the exploitation of human beings for profit. We find ourselves trapped in this system.

After the BP oil spill, I thought deeply about petroleum. The industrial economy treats oil as a resource free for the taking, with a price based only on the cost of extraction and delivery. It shaped a world which became completely dependent on cheap oil. But we had passed the time when oil could be easily extracted, and riskier and dirtier methods were required. Deep sea drilling like that which caused the spill. Tar sands mining in Alberta Canada that destroys the forest, and devastates the health of the people and animals of the region. I knew burning oil for fuel would increase greenhouse gases and bring our climate closer to the brink of disastrous changes. I knew we had to stop burning oil.

But then I took stock of my own life. Our home was heated by oil. I drove a car than ran on gasoline made from oil to buy food and other needed items, and also to go back and forth to the congregation I served. It would take several hours to walk to these destinations from my house, and there was no public transportation nearby. The whole structure of suburban life was dependent upon oil. My congregation is a suburban congregation, and almost every person who came to worship drove there in an automobile. Without oil, it is likely the church, and my house, would not have been built in those locations. The whole geographic structure of our society had been shaped by oil.

But not only that—many material goods in my life were also fabricated from oil. Plastics are made from petroleum, and there was plastic in every room in our house. I wrote on a computer with plastic components. Alarm clocks, toothbrushes, synthetic fabrics, telephones, televisions—all from oil. Modern agriculture is dependent on fertilizer made from oil, and machines that use oil, and a transportation system that uses oil. The asphalt on our roads is made from oil. If oil disappeared tomorrow, the whole system would collapse. And eventually, oil *will* run out. That is one of the realities we are learning in our time. I know we have to change.

But I did not have the ability to undo my own dependence on oil. I could imagine some partial solutions—in fact, they existed already. I imagined driving an electric car and using solar panels to charge up its batteries. I imagined living in a "zero-carbon" house that actually generated more energy than it used. But these options were prohibitively expensive, far beyond my financial means.

So each time I drove a car, or turned on the heat, if I was paying attention, there was a kind of sadness that enveloped me. I felt disappointed and angry that I couldn't just make good ecological choices. Despite my values and idealism about how I wanted to live on the earth, despite how much time I might put into research, it seemed impossible to find workable and affordable choices.

My options as an individual are closely tied to what our society chooses do with its resources. And even if I were able to create a partial personal solution—even if I could afford a zero-carbon home from which I could walk to every necessary function of my life—oil companies would still be breaking open the earth in Alberta, and spilling oil into the Gulf of Mexico. The children living near refineries would still be getting asthma. The ice of the arctic would still be melting, and thousands of species going extinct each year. It breaks my heart.

Ecologist philosopher Joanna Macy teaches that we must honor our pain for the earth. We must not push it away, or pathologize it, or shortchange what it has to teach us. She reminds us, "Don't be afraid of the anguish you feel, or the anger or fear, for these responses arise from the depth of your caring and the truth of your interconnectedness with all beings."[61] Our grief for the earth is part of the cycle of healing, one more way we wake up to our connection to all of life. If we can feel our grief for the earth, we have the capacity to stay awake during these difficult times.

One summer day, caught in this chasm between my hopes for the earth and the choices I saw available to me, I went outside to share my sorrow with the trees and the green plants. I sat down on a blanket and let my pain and brokenness spill over onto the ground. I wanted human society to be better than it is—I wanted there to be a path forward that was not so lonely and hard, so expensive and out of reach. I felt angry with those who are continuing to destroy the earth as if nothing is wrong. I called for help to the four sacred elements of life: the Earth, the Air, the Fire, the Water. They were kinder than I expected.

The Earth said, "Forgive the people of your society. Don't hate your own kind. They didn't know the oil would run out. They were creating what seemed to be good with all this abundance. It's not evil to use oil. It is evil to fight wars and oppress workers and sully the waters in your attempts to secure it and keep it." The Air reminded me, "The songs of birds can dispel sadness, and awaken joy and beauty." The Fire surrounded me with the warmth of love, and said "These energy issues can only be resolved through your connection to the sun. All of our energy comes from the sun." The Water said, "Weep when you are sad. Don't always try to fix it."

And so eventually, that morning, I came to an understanding and acceptance of the challenge that faced me. In order to be alive in this world, I need to grieve and I also need to embrace the messiness of what is, as it is now. I need to accept that human beings as a species do not live in harmony with the earth right now. We are broken off. In order to do the work of healing, of reconnection to the earth, I need to have compassion for myself and my people.

When I feel despair, I am tempted to separate myself from what is broken, to separate what I think of as good from what is bad, identify the saints and the sinners. I am tempted to retreat—to find a community of like-minded souls, grow our own food, live off the grid, leave behind the chaos and destruction of the larger society. Or it may be more subtle—I may want to connect only with people who share my values and ideals, and stop talking to those who seem to be unenlightened. After all, I say, I am on the right side of a very great battle. I am tempted to draw a circle around myself to try to achieve some sort of individual harmony and balance.

But that would cut me off, into another brokenness of separation. Just as I must welcome all the parts of my self, I must welcome all the parts of the larger whole. If I am a part of the circle of life, so is everyone else. If all people and all beings are connected, then in order to be whole, I must open my heart to that larger whole, to the connections between us. This is at the heart of spiritual practice—to open our hearts to the larger whole of which we are a part.

However, when I open my heart to the whole, I experience more profoundly its brokenness, the ways we hurt each other and our earth, the ways we are not in harmony. I feel more grief. I realize in this tension that there can be no individual salvation. If we want to heal ourselves, we must be healers of our world. If we want to heal our world, we must be connected to the broken people. We must embrace the broken to heal the broken. Relationship is at the heart of everything. To be whole in this time is to *be* broken. Stanley Kunitz has written, "In a murderous time/ the heart breaks and breaks/ and lives by breaking."[62]

I learn a lot about embracing the broken through my relationship with my family. I am the oldest of nine siblings. We are spread out over the country in Michigan, Texas, Montana, West Virginia, and Maine. We have vast disagreements among us—the deep religious and political divisions in the larger country are mirrored in my family. As I have written, several of my siblings had a very hard time when I came out as a lesbian and a feminist. It went against everything they believed, and they were appalled by my choices and worried for my soul.

Even so, I helped at the home birth of one sister's second child, and spent three weeks with her family, getting to know her three-year-old during that time. I did not have children of my own, and it was a treasure to begin a connection with these nieces. Since I lived far away, visiting at her home was the best way to nurture those relationships. But when the oldest turned seven, my sister wrote me a letter saying I could no longer stay with them, because she did not want them to be exposed to my beliefs or my identity. Two years later, I finally answered that letter, sharing my sadness and pain about her decision, but the distance continued between us.

On one level, we pretended everything was okay during the few times we were at family events, but inside, my heart was grieving. But then, seven years later, when we were both traveling to West Virginia with our families to visit my parents on the occasion of my dad's birthday, some healing happened. Our division on issues of faith and values and politics had not changed. But my sister wrote me a letter before the visit and asked forgiveness for our nine-year estrangement. She wrote, "Even though I disagree with you about many things, it was wrong of me to cast you out of my life."

When we arrived, we gave each other a hug; later during the visit we were tentatively sharing herbal tea remedies for the allergies we have in common. There were many other poignant moments of connection with family during that visit. My conservative parents warmly welcomed my partner Margy into our gathering. We had fun together: a picnic in the woods, swimming in the pool, and a game of croquet on a hill with two five year olds.

My sister's older daughters, who had been seven and four when I last spent time with them, were now sixteen and thirteen. They had no memory of my earlier visits, and there was no way to recover those nine years of separation. That loss is an emptiness I will continue to carry in my heart. But if I can accept it, I can still find joy in seeing them as young women. And, one evening, when my sister was going out, she asked me to take care of her 18-month-old toddler. The little one was learning the names of things. I followed her around the house as she pointed out to me the fish, the dog, the cat, the ducks, and the eyes on the fish and the tail of the fish, and the eyes on the dog, and—well, you get the idea. It's all a new adventure to her. An open door.

It has been tempting, especially with my family, to get hurt or scared or frustrated and want to shut the doors of my heart. I have to make a choice each day—to listen respectfully, to speak honestly, to be present as myself with those who sometimes don't know what to make of me. I have to forgive them for not being the people I wanted them to be, and open my heart to the people they really are. And wondrously, they are doing the same with me. When I am with them, I feel my heart break wide open—and I wonder, perhaps *God* is big enough to hold all of our experiences, each one of us.

At the edge between the wholeness of our vision and the brokenness we experience there is a place of transformation, if only we can learn how to keep our balance on that edge. There are many temptations that can threaten our balance: retreat, or judgment, or perfectionism, the ever-dangerous shadow sides of visionary idealism. We can even be derailed by the fierce conflicts that rise up within circles of people who care passionately about healing the world.

When I was part of the Women's Peace Camp, we slept in tents, and cooked over wood fires in pits in the ground. We stayed outside on the land most of the day. As part of our protest against the nuclear weapons at the Seneca Army Depot, we were imagining a new way of living that did not require weapons of mass destruction. We consciously developed egalitarian and peaceful ways to be in community with each other, and with the land on which we camped. It was a powerful life-changing experience for me and for many of the women who participated.

But who could have guessed how many conflicts would arise within a group of such like-minded visionary women? One example was the question of appropriate tactics for our protests against the Depot. Some believed non-violent action could include civil disobedience in a classic sense—that one might break a law on behalf of a higher good, done openly, and bearing full responsibility for the consequences of breaking that law. However, others were passionate about symbolic direct action that included cutting the boundary fence of the Depot or going over the fence to spray-paint peace slogans on its buildings in the middle of the night. But even the women who disagreed with such actions were suspect when the police came onto the land to investigate a breach.

Although what any woman did had consequences for every woman at the camp, we had different approaches to the question of how to make such choices and decisions. One group felt all decisions should be sorted out in meetings and a consensus reached before we took action. Others felt we should be free to act in whatever way conscience led, without consultation with anyone else. It became easy to imagine that other women were the problem, rather than the nuclear weapons across the fence.

There is no utopia in which we can leave behind our brokenness. In the very midst of our common vision and our brightest ideals, we bring our full and wounded selves to the table. I have seen this in every community to which I have given my energy, from the Catholic Worker to the Women's Peace Camp, from organizations working for ecological sustainability to religious congregations. Our friends can sometimes break our hearts more deeply than our enemies.

To keep our balance, we must be rooted in compassion and forgiveness. Forgiveness of others for the failures we see in them, the ways people betray the ideals we hold dear, and hurt and wound each other. And forgiveness for ourselves, when we too are unable to live up to our values and ideals, which happens almost every day. Only when we can forgive, can we keep our hearts open, keep hold of the dreams we cherish, keep hope alive.

After all, what do I learn from the natural world? The sun shines down on all of us, despite our brokenness. Its light is constant, never changing because of ideology or virtue, but merely following the rhythm of the seasons and the turning of the world, lighting up the blue sky or the gray clouds. It shines every day, making no distinction between the good and the bad, making no distinction between when I am in tune with my values or when I fail. It warms my face. It gives life to all creatures. The sun teaches me about forgiveness and connection.

And truly, even our brokenness, even our limitations, can become doorways into connection. We are incomplete without each other. We each hold only one small piece of the puzzle. Alone, all we see are jagged edges and random colors. And maybe all together we see just a jumbled pile of jagged pieces—but sometimes we catch a glimpse of the larger picture—what we might become all together. And sometimes, we find another piece that fits together with our own jagged edge. We have to find our joy in each moment of connection.

Significantly, the day after my painful rumination about petroleum in our lives, the newspaper had a story about people building new zero-carbon homes in New England. If I can expand my perspective from my individual options to our collective journey, I can be joyful that some people are creating zero-carbon homes. Something is awakening among human beings that can lead to greater wholeness with the earth.

Our jagged edges teach us we need each other. When I reach the limits of my knowledge or ability, it is a gift to reach out to another person, whose knowledge and ability might balance my own. One day, when I was weary and sad about my recurring impulse to tell my partner what to do, Margy said, "I know you can be controlling sometime, but I love you just the way you are."

We must embrace the jagged edges, embrace the broken pieces. Forgive and be forgiven. This is the path to wholeness. We must hold each other and all beings tenderly, for we are one.

PRACTICE

Get a piece of string, go outside
and make a circle on the ground about three feet in diameter.
(Or, alternatively, get a blanket that can be placed on the ground
to serve as your "circle" space.)
Sit down in the circle,
and imagine the circle is a place of perfect safety and beauty.
Take time to notice all you observe
within the boundaries of the circle.
Now, look beyond the circle,
and notice the beauty of the earth around you.
After a few minutes of appreciation,
let your awareness turn to the brokenness you experience
in the larger circles of your life,
and the brokenness of the earth in this time.
Keep breathing deeply,
and notice the feelings that come up for you.
Name and honor any feelings you feel.
Now, imagine your heart opening up
and expanding beyond your small circle,
reaching out to contain all the beauty
and the brokenness of the earth.

Take time to name the beauty
and the brokenness that enters your heart.
Let yourself feel all the interconnections.
When you are ready,
return your awareness to your small circle.
Feel the ground beneath you
and the sun shining on your skin.
Let yourself feel that light upon you just as you are now.
When you are ready to finish,
step outside the circle saying these words:
I embrace the wide circle of life, both beautiful and broken.
I open my heart to this moment.

13: Stolen Lands, Stolen Children

If we invite the earth to be our teacher, if we want to restore our connection to this land, eventually we must uncover the deep fissures that have devastated this continent. This land was stolen from the Indigenous peoples who belong here, and so many of the children of this land were also stolen away from their homes. We cannot make an authentic relationship to the land without reckoning with these catastrophes. All of us are affected, whether or not we are aware of it. And mainstream culture makes a major effort to keep us unaware.

When my siblings and I were growing up, our mother told us she was part Indian. That was all she knew. But it was enough to open in my heart a curiosity toward Indigenous peoples. As a young adult I tentatively began to learn more about American Indian political struggles, and tried to take what action I could in solidarity. I was able to research our family history to discover that we were distantly related to the Innu people, who are indigenous to the land now called Quebec and Labrador. The French settlers called them *Montagnais*. I learned that the Innu know their land as *Nitasinnan*, which means *our land*.

It is important to acknowledge that my connection to these Innu ancestors does not mean I am Indigenous or Indian. My grandmothers were assimilated into the white community, first in Quebec, and then in the United

States when my grandmother Yvonne came to live in Detroit. Assimilation itself was part of the long campaign to divide Indigenous people from their land and their history. I am a white woman. But some part of me began to feel the history of suffering that otherwise is kept hidden from us in mainstream culture.

Every October and November in the United States, we find ourselves once again in a season of false and misleading stories about European settlers and Native Americans. First there is the story that Columbus discovered America in 1492. Then there is the story about the Pilgrims and the Indians at the first Thanksgiving. It is astonishing to me, after all the work done by Native activists and their allies in the last forty years, that these stories keep returning unchanged year after year. In 1991, the organization Rethinking Schools published *Rethinking Columbus,*[63] an excellent resource that pointed out for educators the fallacies of the stories we are told and offered practical alternatives. Certainly in some places a lot has changed. But there has also been a backlash. *Rethinking Columbus* was one of the books banned from Arizona school systems in 2012.

Perhaps many people are willing to acknowledge, if pressed, that when Columbus supposedly "discovered" America, it was already full of people. But the use of the word "discover" has a more sinister history that is not so often talked about. Prior to 1492, European church leaders and monarchs had collaborated in a stunning series of proclamations, which became known as the Doctrine of Discovery.[64]

In 1452, Pope Nicholas V issued a papal bull declaring that the Catholic king of Portugal had the right to conquer any Muslim and pagan peoples and enslave them. A few years later he wrote a second letter, declaring all the Christian kings of Europe had the right to take the lands and possessions of any non-Christian people, and keep them in perpetuity. If the pagan inhabitants could be converted to the Christian faith they might be spared, but otherwise they could be enslaved or killed. The Doctrine of Discovery was also later claimed by the king of England in 1496, authorizing English explorers to seize any lands not already discovered by other Christian nations.

The Doctrine of Discovery became the legal basis for the "discoveries" of Columbus and others, and for the resulting attempts to conquer and colonize the western hemisphere, and unleash a genocide on its peoples. It was also the legal basis for the slave trade. And its influence did not remain in that distant past. It is still a source of oppression to this day. It became the basis of U.S. Indian Law, beginning in 1823, when Chief Justice John Marshall ruled that "Christian people" who had "discovered" the lands of "heathens" had assumed the right of "dominion," and thus had "diminished" the Indians' rights to complete sovereignty as independent nations. He claimed Indians had merely a right of occupancy in their lands. This decision has never been overturned, and is still cited on a regular basis, as recently as 2010 in the Federal courts.[65]

Responding to the requests of Indigenous peoples, several religious denominations have passed resolutions to repudiate the Doctrine of Discovery. Those of which I am aware are Episcopalians in 2009, Unitarian Universalists and the Society of Friends in 2012, and the United Church of Christ in 2013. These resolutions are a first step toward reckoning with this history of stolen lands and stolen children.

But let's go back to Columbus. The stories of his "discovery" lead to another distortion of our European history in these lands. This is the idea that the Europeans conquered the Native nations by their superior weaponry and military might. This holds a partial truth. The Europeans did try to conquer every Indigenous nation they encountered. But it would not have been possible without another factor. Between 1492 and 1650, possibly ninety percent of the Indigenous people of the Americas were killed by plague and other European diseases to which they had no immunity. The Europeans, sometimes unwittingly but often purposefully, brought an unprecedented apocalypse to this land.

Estimates of the pre-contact population are hard to determine. One scholar, William Denevan, tried to reconcile all the data and came up with fifty-four million in the Western Hemisphere.[66] But by 1650, the number had shrunk to six million. Millions upon millions of people died. In 1617, a few years before English settlers landed, an epidemic began to spread through the area that became southern New England. It likely came from British fishermen, who had been fishing the waters off the coast for decades. By 1620, ninety to ninety-six percent of the population had died. Villages were left with so many bodies, the survivors fled to the next town, and the disease continued to spread. It was a catastrophe never before seen anywhere in the world.[67]

It is hard even to imagine. It decimated the tribes, and left many of their villages empty. One of those villages was Patuxet. When the English settlers arrived in Plymouth Harbor they found a cleared village, with fields recently planted in corn. This was a big part of the reason they chose it for their settlement. All of the village's people had died from the epidemic, except for Tisquantum, whom we know as Squanto. We never really hear the whole story about Squanto either. We hear he taught the settlers how to plant corn and fish and hunt the local area. When I first heard that, I remember wondering how it was he spoke English.

Well, here is the story as told by James W. Loewen.

> As a boy, along with four Penobscots, he was probably stolen by a British captain in about 1605 and taken to England. There he probably spent nine years, two in the employ of a Plymouth merchant who later helped to finance the Mayflower. At length, the merchant helped him arrange a passage back to Massachusetts. He was to enjoy home life for less than a year, however. In 1614, a British slave raider seized him and two dozen fellow Indians and sold them into slavery in Malaga, Spain. Squanto escaped from slavery, ...made his way back to England, and in 1619 talked a ship captain into taking him along [as a guide] on his next trip to Cape Cod.
>
> ... Squanto walked to his home village, only to make the horrifying discovery that... "he was the sole member of his village still alive. All the others had perished in the epidemic two years before."[68]

Perhaps this was why he was willing to help the Plymouth Colony which had settled in his people's village. Another theory holds he was sent there by the Wampanoag leader, Massasoit, to keep an eye on them. It was a depleted and downhearted people who had survived the epidemics. Perhaps they thought it might prove beneficial to make an alliance with these newcomers.

The settlers, too, lost half their people during the first hard winter. There were only fifty-three settlers who survived until the harvest festival that was later declared to be the first Thanksgiving. One theory suggests when the settlers sent out men to hunt for fowl for the feast, the Wampanoags heard the gunfire and went to investigate. Massasoit and ninety of his men arrived. Seeing a harvest festival going on, they went out hunting and brought back five deer as a gift, and they all ate together and visited for three days.

It was a brief moment of tentative peace. One generation later, the English settlers and the Wampanoag were at war. For many Native people in our time, the day called Thanksgiving has become a Day of Mourning, for the hundreds of years of losses suffered by their people.

If European Americans begin to learn the real stories, and become aware of the level of devastation and grief suffered by Indigenous peoples, our first reaction can sometimes be defensiveness. After all, we think, it wasn't me, personally, who stole Indian land, or caused disease among the people, or killed anyone. Perhaps our second reaction is a feeling of guilt, because of what our ancestors may have done. But I have learned that neither defensiveness nor guilt is really very helpful. In a way, they keep the overwhelming losses at arm's length. We must go deeper than that. Is there a way we can acknowledge the terrible brokenness? How can we begin to find healing, or a way to restore wholeness?

One first step for me has been to listen to Indigenous people tell their own stories. I needed to learn how to listen to stories of loss and pain. Listening is not about fixing something, or feeling guilty, or giving advice. Listening is about being present and opening our hearts to the experience of someone who has a story to tell. We need to seek out those stories of brokenness, listen and let our hearts be broken by them. There have been moments when the pain of such listening has felt almost too much to bear, but I reminded myself how much more painful it must be for the one telling the story. Then I felt such gratitude that someone was willing to share these stories with us.

Let me tell you about one opportunity that used listening to create a path to healing. In the fall of 2012, I attended a presentation about the Maine Wabanaki Child Welfare Truth and Reconciliation Commission. The goals of the commission were three: to find out and write down what happened to Wabanaki people involved with the Maine child welfare system; to give Wabanaki people a place to share their stories, to have a voice and to heal; and, to give the Maine child welfare system guidance on how it can work better with Wabanaki people[69].

The history underlying this effort is soul shattering. One of the ways the U.S. and Canadian governments tried to solve their so-called "Indian problem" was to take Indian children away from their families and communities. Beginning in the 1800s, children were taken from their homes and sent to boarding schools run by different churches. The purpose was to destroy their Indian identity, and assimilate them into a white way of being. Their hair was cut and their own clothing was taken away. They were forbidden to speak their languages, or practice their religions, and often did not see their parents again for years. This original horror was amplified by emotional, physical, and sexual abuse. Many children died. Those who made it home were not the same as when they left.

In the 1950s and 60s, the Bureau of Indian Affairs and the Child Welfare League of America tried another experiment: they took hundreds of Native children from their families and tribes to give to white families to adopt and raise. Hundreds of others were taken from their homes and placed in white foster care. In Maine, Native children were taken from their families and placed in white foster homes at a higher rate than most other states. The stealing of children has been one of the worst forms of genocidal oppression Indigenous peoples have suffered.

In 1978, after heroic efforts by Native activists, Congress passed the Indian Child Welfare Act. It recognized that children's tribal citizenship is as important as their family relationships. It stipulated that child welfare agencies should work with tribal agencies to keep children within the community, and prioritized placing children with relatives rather than taking them to strangers outside of the community. They also recognized that there is "no resource that is more vital to the continued existence and integrity of Indian tribes than their children."[70]

The effects of stealing the children persist through generations of Native families and communities. Co-founder of the Truth and Reconciliation Commission, Passamaquoddy Denise Altvater, spoke of how she had been taken to foster care as a seven-year-old child.

> State workers came onto the reservation. My five sisters and I were home. My mother was not home. They took all of our belongings and they put them in garbage bags. They herded us into station wagons and drove us away for a long, long time…
>
> They took us to a state foster home in the Old Town area and left us there for four years. During those four years, our foster parents sexually assaulted us. They starved us. They did some horrific things to us.[71]

No one believed them when they tried to get help. During another three years they were placed in kinder situations, but the dislocation and sense of not belonging anywhere caused lasting psychic trauma.[72] In adulthood, even though Denise eventually became successful in a career and was admired by many, this trauma left her feeling a profound sense of disconnection. She did not know how to be a real parent to her children, and she saw its effects in the struggles of her children and granddaughter.[73]

Telling these stories is incredibly painful. Denise Altvater revealed that she had a breakdown after she first shared her story. But she persevered because being able to speak the truth is central to the path toward healing. Without her willingness to tell her story, the Truth and Reconciliation Commission might never have come to be. Listening to her story, I felt my heart break open, too, for the hurt caused to those young ones who were so vulnerable, for the pain that repeated itself through generations.

Denise and others who were working to implement the Indian Child Welfare Act in Maine, educating state workers about its meaning and implications, realized they needed a process to deal with the deep levels of hurt and trauma Native people and communities were carrying. The Truth and Reconciliation Commission hoped to be a tool for that healing, and for making changes so children are not suffering in the future what they suffered in the past.[74]

The mandate for the Commission was signed by Tribal leaders from the five Wabanaki communities in Maine and by the governor of Maine. Five commissioners were selected and community support was set up for those who told their stories. This was the first Truth and Reconciliation of its kind in the United States. Organizers also established a network of non-Native allies to lend support to the Commission's process.

Healing becomes possible through telling the stories and through listening to the stories. Healing becomes possible through re-building trust and connection between Native and non-Native peoples. When we listen together, there is hope. Native people want us to move beyond myths and stereotypes and learn more deeply and accurately about the issues they face today. Those of us living in the mainstream society can use our advantage and position to be allies and resources for Native peoples' concerns, and to join together in our common concerns for the earth.

In her novel, *Solar Storms*, Chickasaw writer Linda Hogan begins with a story of an unusual feast given by a woman named Bush. Bush was grieving the loss of a small child, Angel, after she was taken away from their tiny Native community by the white county authorities. Though not related by blood, Bush had cared for Angel after Angel's mother could not. In order to reckon with her grief, Bush prepared food for the whole community, and then she gave away all of her possessions to them. Hogan writes, in the voice of one who had been to the feast:

> Going back that morning, in the blue northern light, their stomachs were filled, their arms laden with blankets, food... But the most important thing they carried was Bush's sorrow. It was small now, and child-sized, and it slid its hand inside theirs and walked away with them. We all had it, after that. It became our own. Some of us have since wanted to give it back to her, but once we felt it we knew it was too large for a single person. After that your absence sat at every table, occupied every room, walked through the doors of every house.[75]

By this sharing of sorrow, the sorrow became bearable. Indigenous people are too often bearing the sorrows of our history alone. Once we let ourselves feel this grief, we realize it is much too large for one people to carry alone. But the more of us who are willing to carry this sorrow, the more of us who are willing to join in the struggle, the more bearable it will be.

PRACTICE

Learn about the peoples
indigenous to the place where you live.
Learn the history and the stories.
Listen.
Find out the current issues
affecting Indigenous people who live nearby.
Find out if there are ways to be an ally
in the work on those issues.
Get involved, respectfully.

14: In Search of Belonging

European-descent peoples are new to the land we call America. Our history includes the stealing of this land from its original people. But our history also includes another loss, our own separation from the lands of our ancestors. We are like orphans here. There is a brokenness in this, too.

Lakota chief Luther Standing Bear said, "Men must be born and reborn to belong. Their bodies must be formed of the dust of their forefathers' bones."[76] To be indigenous is to belong to a particular place, through that interweaving of dust and food and intimate knowledge which accumulates over millennia. When I lived in Jamaica Plain, Massachusetts, I used to walk regularly in the Forest Hills Cemetery. It was a beautiful tree-filled park that nourished my spirit, but none of my ancestors were buried there. No familiar ghosts recognized me or called my name. I was not indigenous to that place, nor to any of the places I have lived.

I learned more about what it might mean to be indigenous to a place through Linda Hogan's novel, *Solar Storms*. Her main character, Angel, had been raised in foster care after being abused by her mentally ill mother. At seventeen, she comes searching for her relatives. When she and her grandmothers travel to their ancestral land, something happens for her. "A part of me remembered this world... it seemed to embody us. We were shaped out of this land by the hands of gods. Or maybe it was that we embodied the land. And in some way I could not yet comprehend, it also embodied my mother, both of them stripped and torn."[77]

Angel's family returns to their land in the north of Canada because it is being threatened with hydro-electric development. It is no pristine wilderness or unspoiled scenery to which she is responding. The land is under assault, and they feel a responsibility to fight for its protection. She learns how the bonds between the land and the people have been broken by the developments of many years.

The elder Tulik tells Angel, "...here a person is only strong when they feel the land. Until then a person is not a human being."[78] Angel ponders these words, and comes to realize he is right. "There was a deep intelligence in this, and I, too, was feeling the rhythm of it inside myself. My heart and the beat of the land, the land I should have come from, were becoming the same thing."[79]

Angel's early guardian, Bush, is a Chickasaw from Oklahoma who had married Angel's grandfather. She travels with them to help in the struggle for the land. Angel notices that the land in the far north loves Bush, "but it did not tell her the things it told the rest of us. It kept secrets from her."[80] Even though Bush is Native American, she is not indigenous to that particular land. Through these nuances, I began to better understand how connecting to the earth is not just about belonging to a continent, or loving the land in some generic way, but must develop through our relationship to a particular river, a particular valley or hill or peninsula.

For several years, I was active as an ally to the Cree, Inuit, and Innu peoples in their struggle against hydroelectric development in Northern Quebec. The electricity from that development was being sold to New England states, where I lived, and allies in New England tried to educate consumers about the destructiveness of large-scale hydropower.

I learned that the traditional way of life for each of the nations included hunting and fishing and gathering. In my imagination, I had envisioned small bands of people roaming over vast wilderness at random, looking for game. But the reality was different. Each small family band had very specific territory—certain rivers and waterways, certain areas whose terrain was utterly familiar to them. The beavers in that territory were counted by them, and traplines had been set out for generations. When the LaGrande project was built in 1970, those particular beloved lands were flooded and lost to them, with their ancestors' graves, their memories and stories of love and new life and home. I learned even the migrating birds return to the very sedges from which they had departed the previous season. They, like the Cree, had lost their homes.

Lakota scholar Vine Deloria writes about some of the distinctions between European-American ways of thinking and American Indian ways of thinking. One important difference is a primary orientation towards time versus a primary orientation toward place.[81] Europeans are focused on time, he says, and understand the world as an evolutionary process where humankind evolved from lower forms into higher forms, including the evolution from so-called primitive religions into monotheistic conceptions of divinity. I remember learning about something similar in Catholic grade school called *salvation history*—the idea that *God* worked throughout time to bring humans into a higher level of understanding.

American Indians are more focused on place, and their theological concerns are spacial concerns. Within this framework, each place has its own experiences of divinity, which may be very different from those of other places, without conflict or contradiction among those differences. Rituals are important for connecting a people with the place in which they live, with the deeper powers of that place. This is why the struggles of Native people for religious freedom cannot be separated from their struggle for land rights. Their religions nurture their relationship to the specific land which is their land.

Another difference between European-American society and the views of American Indians is their conception of land as object or subject.[82] Mainstream society views the land as an object to be acted upon—to be bought and sold, to be harvested for its plants and minerals, to be owned, or even to be watched over carefully. Indians view the land as a subject, seeing it in the same way a person is viewed, as a being with its own activity, its own viewpoint, its own intentions, its own dignity.

The word *own* is a puzzling one here. We use it to describe possession acquired by buying something. As in "I own a piece of property." Yet it can also be used to describe relationship. My own mother, my own lover, my own family. To say "our own land" can mean this is the land we have purchased, or it can mean this is the land to which we have a relationship, we belong to it as much as it belongs to us.

The more I have learned about what it means to be indigenous, the more I am aware how broken is the relationship between myself and the land, my people and the land. I remember watching James Cameron's movie *Avatar*, where the people of the planet Pandora were connecting to a living tree in a sort of psychic neural net of communication. I started sobbing after the movie, somehow realizing I would never experience that kind of connection to my own planet. Something in me was too wounded for that. I might be able to restore a level of communication and belonging, but an essential language had been irretrievably lost.

I recently read about a psychological problem called "attachment disorder" in children. It is a controversial diagnosis given to some adopted children who, because of severe abandonment or abuse in their early years, become unable to form attachments with their new families. Children need to be loved and held and cared for; they need to be connected to their caregivers in order to thrive. Without that connection, they can become deeply wounded beings.

I wonder if perhaps we European-American people are suffering from an "attachment disorder" in regard to the earth. Perhaps the bond we should have had with the land was destroyed again and again from generation to generation, until we don't even realize what real connection might feel like. Most of us are no longer aware of what we lack.

I don't think our society could do what it does to the land, if it was alive to that connection. How could people destroy a forest, if they felt the bonds that should exist between them and the land? How could we pollute the water or destroy habitat until animals go extinct? It is like killing your mother or your child. There are human beings so damaged they will kill their mother.

But perhaps some of us are damaged like that in the connection we should have with the land on which we live.

What does it mean to feel the land? How do we learn to feel the land, if our history and culture has deprived us of the knowledge of that connection? Perhaps European peoples lost something in the early chapters of their history with their land, and then, arriving on these shores, began systematically to try to break the bonds that existed between Indigenous peoples and their lands, as they continue to do so today.

I am remembering a story I learned in the work of Rebecca Parker and Rita Nakashima Brock. They researched the images in Christian sanctuaries over the last two thousand years and discovered the earliest sanctuaries were filled with beautiful images of the garden: trees, pastoral animals, human figures in an earthly paradise. Only after almost nine hundred years did the image of the crucifix appear. They asked, "Why did Christians turn from a vision of paradise in this life to a focus on the Crucifixion and final judgment?"[83] In their book, *Saving Paradise*, they trace the complex changes—century by century—that might account for such a development.

One story in particular was deeply moving to me. Their trail of clues led to the eighth century, when the Frankish King Charles the Great, better known as Charlemagne, attempted to conquer and annex the Saxon people's lands along the Rhine River. The Saxons had practiced a hybrid form of Christianity, a blending of the Christian story with their earlier pagan practices. Thor and Woden and Jesus were all acknowledged, and their worship was held in sacred groves of oak trees or around holy springs.

The Franks justified their expansionist assaults by claiming the Saxons were not true Christians. They cut down the sacred oak trees, and deforested the whole countryside. They baptized the Saxons under threat of death. The Saxons kept rebelling decade after decade, but ultimately lost the wars. It was the descendants of those embattled Saxons who eventually carved the first crucifix, and later carried out the first European pogrom against the Jews.[84] What does it do to a people to sever their relationship to their land? Did this wounding eventually fuel the colonizers' ferocity to break the Indigenous peoples' bonds in America as well?

My ancestry is three quarters Germanic, and almost one quarter French. These battles live in my DNA. In the early days of my feminist awakening, I began to trace the ancestry of my mother line, to learn who my grandmothers might be, and what land we originally came from. My matrilineal great-great-great-grandmother was an Innu woman. She married a Scottish trapper who worked for the Hudson Bay Company in Quebec. His name was Peter Macleod, and he called her *Marie de Terres Rompues*, after the place where they lived on the Saguenay River. Her name might be translated, *Marie of Broken Lands*. How very prophetic for this search of mine.

When I have been able to travel to Quebec, to the place the Innu call *Nitasinnan*, I have felt the presence of the ghosts of my ancestors in the land. The very first time I drove into Chicoutimi on the Saguenay River, I came upon a book on the shelves of the Welcome Center in the rest area—it was about my ancestor Peter Macleod and his family. There have been other encounters over the years, a feeling of my ancestors reaching out to me as I reach out to them.

Learning about their stories has been an important part of my journey. I discovered the many dislocations and relocations that occurred for my grandmothers, the ways they were separated from the land and people from which they came. *Marie de Terres Rompues* bore several children with Peter MacLeod. Her daughter, Angele, was only twelve when her mother died, and Peter married another wife; Angele's stepmother was a white woman. I wonder if Angele kept a connection to her Innu relatives? She married at the age of twenty to a French Quebecois farmer, Joseph Tremblay, and they lived in the area of Peribonka near Lac St. Jean. I only know one story about them, from a census report. One year, all their grain burned in May, and they replanted with fresh grain but all of it was frozen and "not fit to be threshed."

Her daughter Claudia was only eighteen when Angele died. At twenty-two, Claudia married Ferdinand, and during an economic downturn in their region, they moved over four hundred miles away to the town of Hull in the suburbs of Ottawa. Later, they traveled over seventeen hundred miles to the Black Hills of South Dakota, where Ferdinand worked in the mica mines for five years, during the boom years when Westinghouse Electric was producing over $100,000 per year in mica. Then the mines closed.

Their daughter, my grandmother Yvonne, was born in Hull; she was nine when they moved to the Black Hills, and fourteen when they returned to Quebec. She became a chamber maid in a hotel in the Canadian capital city of Ottawa, where at seventeen she met Johann, an Austrian immigrant working as a waiter. She traveled with him five hundred miles to the United States, marrying at the border in Detroit Michigan.

My mother tells me Yvonne and her sisters didn't want anyone to think they looked Indian. Did she fear prejudice learned in Quebec, or in South Dakota? In Detroit, she was fully assimilated into the white and English world. Most of the stories were lost, but she did tell my mother they were part-Indian, and my mom grew up feeling proud of that heritage. There were very occasional visits to family in Canada. When my mother was a little girl, the news came of Claudia's death at the age of seventy-three.

My mother was only twenty-one when her mother, Yvonne, died. I was a baby then. I have a picture of my grandmother holding me in her arms. When I ponder this story of my mothers and grandmothers, I am struck by how most of these women lost their mothers just as they were entering adulthood. They each turned to the life and the cultures of their husbands. And I am struck by the many miles each generation traveled away from the place in which they might have felt a sense of belonging to the land. My mother, too, followed her husband on his travels across the United States. I grew up during those travels and none of those places ever felt like home. I don't remember feeling sad during those years about not being connected to a place. I didn't know any other way. The sadness came later. But mine is a story not uncommon among people in America.

How do we find our way back? How do we find a sense of belonging to a place, to a particular land, when we have never really known what that feels like? What can help us heal? Ecologist Joanna Macy suggests it might be our grief that wakes us up. I think about my tears after the movie *Avatar*. Perhaps the first step toward connection is the grief that emerges as our disconnection becomes clear. We start to feel the pain that has been covered over for generations. We start to feel the pain of what is happening to the land in our time.

As I began to understand this brokenness, I sometimes felt ashamed about being white, and wished I was part of a tribe, wished I was Indian instead of white. Other white people have felt this too. Native peoples have a name for it—the *Wannabe Tribe*.[85] White society in this day and age romanticizes Indians and Indian culture, even as it hides the devastations it inflicts on them.

One of the troubling manifestations of this romantic longing has been the widespread marketing of so-called "Native American Spirituality." I remember when I and other women were looking for new images and practices to connect with *Mystery*, we were inspired by what we learned about Native religions. Could we find there ways to honor women and to connect to the earth? Could we borrow rituals and practices that had a long history on this continent? At first we didn't understand the larger dangers of taking fragments of Native spiritual practices out of context. But Indigenous women in our communities let us know this was not the answer. They were frustrated and even outraged by this use of their culture and religions.

Janet McCloud, a Tulalip elder and fishing rights activist, says,

> First they came to take our land and water, then our fish and game. ...Now they want our religions as well. All of a sudden, we have a lot of unscrupulous idiots running around saying they're medicine people. And they'll sell you a sweat lodge ceremony for fifty bucks. It's not only wrong, it's obscene. Indians don't sell their spirituality to anybody, for any price. This is just another in a very long series of thefts from Indian people and, in some ways, this is the worst one yet.[86]

The problem of spiritual theft is especially dangerous for those of us who are seeking to reconnect with the earth. One the one hand, we have much to learn from Native peoples about this land and about what it means to honor our relationship to land. We must take our lead from those who have been living in these places for millennia, who have the knowledge that comes from belonging to a place. My own journey would be impossible without the wisdom and philosophy that has been shared by Indigenous peoples. But in our search for help, we can do damage, too, because of the context of the broken bonds between us, because of the ongoing societal process of oppression and colonization.

Indian spiritual traditions are inextricably woven into the network of relationships of an Indian community and of the particular land in which that community lives. Spirituality is a fundamental element of the Native struggle against the destruction of their cultures and homes, perhaps the most important resource for Native peoples to heal their own broken connections with the land and with their ancestors. These traditions are not meant to be exported piecemeal for some other purpose, however earnest it may be.

Non-indigenous people must do our own spiritual work. We all come from ancestors who were indigenous to some place on this planet. Europeans had their own indigenous traditions to connect them to their land, remnants of which survived into Christian times. We see traces of this in our customs even here in this country—the evergreen trees of the winter holidays, the foods we prepare for special times of the year. Part of our journey may involve reclaiming these old European earth traditions.

There is a rune, part of the early Germanic sacred alphabet, called *Othila*, whose meaning pointed to the irrevocable relationship between people and the land on which they live. In Germanic countries, there is still a legal right called the right of *odal*. It means a person living on a particular estate has the right to stay and live on that estate after the owner has died. Love for the earth has hidden roots to be discovered even in our European ancestors' ways.

The reality is that we are still a part of the earth, even though we are broken off from our ancestral places. Indigenous people have a belief that every person and being on this earth are related to each other. We must reweave our own culture's relationship to the earth, even as we seek to restore right relationship with those who have been here before us. We all live here on this land and our lives are equally enmeshed with the fate of countless other beings around us. This land, broken as she is, is our only source of food and water. This land is full of nourishment for us, both material and spiritual.

One summer, I learned that by eating local honey, I could help the hay-fever I suffered from during the summertime. That honey began to make a relationship between my body and the plants that grew near my home. The pollen and nectar of their flowers were gathered by the bees and became infused into my own cells. Eating locally-grown foods is one way to reweave the bond between our bodies and a place. This is the deep reality. It is our encounter with a specific location, the place where we live, which forms a doorway for us to feel the earth, to find a sense of belonging. We can love the earth, and be loved by the earth, even if she keeps some secrets from us.

PRACTICE

Please don't spend your money
on so-called "Native" spirituality workshops.
Don't try to steal someone else's culture.
Do your own spiritual work.
Research the stories of your own ancestors.
Learn their names and their birthplaces.
Trace the journeys that brought them
to the land where you now reside.
Learn the stories of their brokenness and their connections.
Ask them to help you find your way.

15: Seeing in the Dark

One winter night, I went outside after dark. I walked through the snow around the perimeter of our acre of land. I loved how the winter revealed our night visitors. We rarely saw deer in our yard, but their tracks showed us how they passed through on their quiet journeys. I stood beneath the trees gazing at the stars. I was pondering once again in my heart, how can we live on this earth? Can we find a way forward? Then I saw a shooting meteorite streak across the sky. I felt warm in the cold, I felt at home among the trees. I felt a stillness in my heart.

I used to be afraid of the darkness. Women and girls, especially, were taught the darkness is full of dangers. We were told not to walk alone at night, not to go into solitary places. We learned bad things could happen to us there.

All cultures seem to have known some trepidation about the dark of night. There are wild creatures that emerge after the sun goes down, and dangerous hunting animals on the prowl. The shepherds of the Christmas story watched their flocks by night, because otherwise wolves would attack the sheep. The herders were armed with staffs and rods, and kept their dogs close by for protection. Night is cold and hides unknown threats that may be lurking in the shadows.

In the early days of the women's movement, in protest of violence against women, we held marches and vigils to "Take Back the Night." We began to question the logic that we should limit our freedom for the unfulfilled promise of safety. Though we had been taught to fear strangers in the night, we learned that most attacks against women were perpetrated by family members. That which supposedly would protect us, instead was the hidden source of our danger. Additionally, our fear itself imprisoned us and robbed us of the fullness of life.

Now I love the night. But I still feel anxious when I want to go into it alone. One summer I had the idea to sleep overnight in our backyard. We had purchased a screen tent, so we could enjoy being outside without the bugs driving us crazy. We set it up in the far back corner of our yard in a little birch grove. It was the place where the deer emerged to wander through, from an open field on the other side of the trees at that corner. So I thought of it as "where the wild things are."

As I made plans for my night outside, worried thoughts began to bubble up. I said to Margy, "What if a bear comes through?" But she laughed, and said, "There aren't any bears in North Yarmouth." I decided, rather than go outside when it was already dark, it would be easier if I went outside before dusk, and then watched as darkness fell.

So we built a fire in our fire pit, and hung out together for a while, and then Margy went inside and I set up a bamboo pad and sleeping bag in the screen tent. The ground was hard and my muscles ached with the damp and cold, but not overly so. The stars grew bright in the moonless sky. I felt proud of facing my fear, and relished the solitude. The anxieties of my heart seemed to grow smaller and smaller in that deep and mysterious retreat. The singing of birds woke me in the early dawn before the sun rose.

There is a funny sequel to my adventure. Several days later, Margy showed me a clipping from our local paper. It was a picture of a bear, with the following tagline: "A North Yarmouth resident said her family was having breakfast June 25th when this black bear came out of the woods to snack at their bird feeder."[87] I'm glad I didn't see that story before I slept out. Sometimes, there are bears in the darkness.

I first began to explore the night world at women's music festivals. We were camping out on land with thousands of other women, and we felt truly safe to walk about at night. Perhaps more safe than many of us had ever felt. I didn't realize how much it would change me—something shifted in the very way I held my body as I walked.

Later, at the Women's Peace Camp, I camped outside with other women for two entire summers. It was more challenging—there were only about thirty of us, and we were under constant surveillance from the military and occasional harassment from the neighbors. We kept whistles in our tents, to signal to each other if any danger came near us, and we took turns keeping watch at night around a fire. Yet these night watches were not an onerous chore—they were the opportunity for long deep conversations, kindling enduring friendships and sometimes romance. In the quiet of my tent, I became familiar with the night sounds of animals, attentive to distinguish them from the sounds of possible human intruders.

I was also at the Peace Camp with a few others through the winter of 1986, in an old farmhouse with a wood stove and no indoor plumbing. I remember one night I was there alone, and felt insecure and vulnerable. Perhaps it was a time when we were receiving threats from people in the nearby town. I went outside for a while, well-wrapped in snow pants and a warm coat. I sat in the shadows under a tree, and felt safer, there in the dark, watchful and hidden—I was at home with the night creatures, and knew danger was likely to arrive only in a truck or an automobile with lights on.

What do we miss if we don't go outside at night? The quiet, the nocturnal sounds, the change of mood. Darkness invites reflection, memory, story-telling, music, imagination, the unknown. The darkness is the birthplace of mystery and vision. The dark invites us into a peaceful stillness, into listening and wondering, into questions needing no answers.

When I lived in Boston I would go at night with my women's spirituality group into the Blue Hills south of the city. We'd climb to the top of a particular hill we called Blueberry Hill, and gather around a fire under the stars, up where we could see all the way to the lights of the city and the waters of the harbor. We had learned about something called *wraith* energy, an energy imbued in the fertile soil, the mist, the plants and trees. To be outside in the dark was to be filled with this energy. One night, the fog came in as we were finishing our ritual, and we couldn't see anything below the top of the hill. But we knew the way home was down, and so we let our feet find a path, like Capricorn goats walking in single file.

Just so, as we seek to regain our connections to the earth, the way home is a downward path. We have to let our feet find the trail in a kind of foggy darkness in which we cannot discern clearly the road before us. In Siberia and Mongolia, the word *shaman* means one who sees in the dark.[88] We were seeing in the dark that night, walking down the hill in the fog. The shamans of the northern peoples were the healers, the teachers. They lived in a world where the winter sun would disappear for weeks at a time. In the dark, they sought out the ancestors and the animals, to hunt for guidance for their people.

As we look for direction in our time, we need to be willing to enter the darkness, to venture into the unknown. We can't figure this out with merely the light of intellect and reason. We need to go into the dark to be led into a new way we have not seen before.

In our culture, light is idealized and dark is devalued—they are set up as great enemies. The war of light against dark is a metaphor undergirding other great dichotomies: good and evil, sacred and secular, male and female, white and black—dichotomies that perpetuate fundamentalism, racism, and oppression.

We create an artificial extension of our daytime with electric lights—these lights shine throughout the night, and we don't have to stop working and doing. But human beings are biologically designed for cycles of wake and sleep, light and dark, work and dreaming. The dark is not lost time—it is the time of healing, of weaving our experience into the fabric of memories, of balance and beginnings, of loving and touching.

Even sitting in the dark inside our houses can open up new forms of knowing. I remember an evening when a few friends had gathered in my living room. We sat in the dark with only one candle lit, just quietly talking, and we began to share our despair for the world. We moved from despair to inspiration and found ideas rising like sparks in the play of shadows and light, ideas about how we would take action on behalf of peace. It never feels like a meeting when the lights are out. Try it sometime. Notice how your conversations grow deeper and more whimsical.

The dark has been a metaphor for what we fear—death, loss, sadness, despair. But the dark is also the fertile ground for imagination and discovery. For something unknown to be revealed, we need that stillness, that quiet whisper, that letting go of action and control. The dark is the time for asking deep questions, like, why are we here, and where are we going? It is the time to "imagine a great presence stirring beside" us.[89]

To become whole, we need the darkness as much as we need the light. Dark and light are not enemies, but dancers in a unified rhythm. Embracing the dark also reminds me to welcome back everything we may have rejected—the shadow side of our consciousness. We must welcome the shadow in order to find the depths of wisdom and healing. When we embrace the darkness, we shift our interior map, and expand its parameters.

In the daylight, we can see only one star, our sun, and the earth in its perennial relationship. But in the dark, we can see the universe. Our vision expands exponentially. The darkness also expands past vision into different ways of perceiving and knowing, into dream land, into what cannot be expressed. Perhaps it is here we can find our roots in the ground, the soil, the ancient ways our peoples once knew to read the non-verbal language of the land. So much more is unknown than known. In the dark we find intuition, surrender, mystical union, we find what cannot be spoken or counted. If I want to learn the language of the earth, it may sound like silence.

It is also so beautiful just to sit outside on a dark night and look up. In the dark we can see the stars. Can you imagine what it might be like if there were no stars to see? If the sky was merely a curtain of black? How much would be lost of dreaming and wonder. How alone we might feel.

For millennia, our ancestors have watched the stars, followed the rising and setting of the moon and the planets. Without the dark, they would not have discovered our place in the universe, the circling of the planets and comets and meteors, and the movement of the earth around the sun. They would not have learned the secrets of the far away galaxies and the origins of space and time.

Ancient peoples told stories about the stars, and grouped them into patterns, called constellations, naming them after their *Gods* and heroes. They were especially fascinated by those stars that lay within the track of the planets and the moon and sun, called the zodiac. Many cultures told stories of ancestors who had come from the Milky Way. Different cultures told different stories—but they all had stories about the stars.

They also had incredible practical knowledge. The Mayan priests, for example, wrote down their observations and created a calendar that was extremely accurate. It predicted eclipses of the sun and the path of Venus all within a margin of error of one day in over 6000 years. In other cultures, sailors used the stars to plot their course across the seas. We have lost a huge amount of that widespread common star knowledge. I remember how excited I was to learn you could tell what time it was by the rotation of constellations around the North Star. I know how to figure out the directions by finding the North Star. I wonder how many modern people have lost even that.

The ancient peoples saw omens and forces at work in the sky, that might shape our personalities and our destinies. Whether we believe in it or not, their ways of mapping and interpreting the sky have endured even into the present day. A fair number of us know our astrological signs, though probably only a few can find the corresponding constellations in the sky.

In our time, though we aren't so intimately familiar with visible stars of the night sky, we have seen wonders the ancients did not even dream about. The Hubble telescope orbiting the earth has recorded images from almost the very limits of the visible universe, 13 billion light years away, and 13 billion years old. We can see photos of nebulae, black holes, supernovas, and star nurseries, just by looking online.

It was only in 1996 that astronomers first found evidence of a planet orbiting a star beyond our solar system. Now, astronomers have identified more than five hundred. With two to four hundred billion stars in our Milky Way galaxy, and one to five hundred billion galaxies, some estimates suggest there are at least ten trillion planetary systems in the universe. Curiosity, wonder, vastness beyond imagining. We dream, we hope, we want to believe we are not alone. The stars give us that. In many languages, including the ancient Greek of the Bible, the word for sky is the same as the word for heaven.

When I let my imagination ponder the vast expanses of space, the billions of stars and planets, both seen and unseen, it makes the top of my head fly off. Everything else that might be going on starts to seem so small. We are merely specks in the universe. And yet we are specks that can look at the night sky, and build telescopes to explore this vast beauty and mystery.

The thing is—if it weren't for the darkness, we would never know about the stars. Writer Annie Dillard tells us, "You do not have to sit outside in the dark. If, however, you want to look at the stars, you will find that darkness is necessary. But the stars neither require nor demand it."[90] The stars are there all the time. They wait invisibly in the daytime. But in the depths of the night, they reveal themselves. They awaken mystery and wonder and hope and imagination.

If we never go into the dark, we cannot see what we need to see, when troubles come to our families and to our world. In the dark, we find what we cannot imagine in the daylight. In the dark we see the stars. In the dark we might see the bigger picture. In the dark, what is unknown may reveal itself to us. There is more out there than we already know.

PRACTICE

Take a walk in the dark without a flashlight.
Bring a friend if you feel afraid,
but don't talk aloud to each other.
Be still at first if you need to,
and let your eyes adjust to the light of the stars and moon.
See if your feet can feel the ground of the path or road
on which you are walking.
Go slowly, and listen to the night noises around you.
Bring to the dark your deepest questions, your biggest troubles.
Don't try to think about the answers.
Watch the stars and let the unknown universe respond.
Be very quiet as you slowly walk back home.

16: The Language of Trees

One day when I was walking through the Forest Hills cemetery I came across a beautiful old copper beech tree. It was about ten minutes from my home in Jamaica Plain, and was situated next to a small pond. I called it the four directions tree. This was because its giant trunk divided into four huge branches at about the level of my waist, and then reached toward the sky in opposite directions. One of the branches bent off a little lower, so it served as a step, up to a spot where a person could sit, right in the heart of the tree.

Almost every day after that I would climb up to that perch, and lean my back against the smooth gray bark. From within, the purple leaves of the tree appeared a luminescent green as the sun's light filtered through. Some of the branches bent downward to almost touch the earth again, creating a shady yet glowing canopy. On the gray bark all around me were carved initials and messages—ragged names and dates, hearts and promises of true love always. I used to be upset people would carve on trees, but then I began to wonder if there was something about these particular trees with their smooth elephant-like skins, that invited us to leave a permanent record.

When I was feeling tired or anxious, I would sit in the four directions tree and give it my worries. Sometimes I felt if a moment were important enough, I too would want to carve my tale in letters in its bark. My sisters and I, when we were little, would take turns writing words on each others' backs as we lay in bed at night. The one whose back was being written on would try to read what message was being spelled out. I wondered if maybe, in a very important moment, the tree might read my words like that.

The beech tree helped me to feel grounded, its solid trunk and branches were something to rely on: when my days got too hectic and it seemed I would never finish everything I had to do; when I was anxious about my future and wondered if I would find my calling; when I grew discouraged about the struggle and pain of the world around me. Whenever I found myself speeding up—as if I were on a frantic chase that left me breathless, as if I were trying to catch up to something just out of reach.

Then, I would go to the four directions tree. The tree didn't speak in English words. But it seemed to bring me answers in a more subtle language. I would trace its bark with my fingertips, and remember who I was. I would remember that speeding up never brings me more time; only slowing down can do that.

I never did carve my initials there, but it seemed as if my deepest identity could be deciphered in its patterns. Sitting with my back against one of the branches, I could feel myself growing roots. I could feel myself become as common as soil. As precious as water. Worthy of the sun. Perhaps that is the secret of why we write on trees. So our truest dreams and memories might be found there again and again.

When I sat in that old tree, surrounded by the hopeful carvings of many human persons, I was reminded of the runes, the early carved alphabet of the Germanic languages. I had taken up the study of runes, because I was curious about the culture and spirituality of my ancient Germanic ancestors on my father's side of the family. The traditional way of making runes is to carve them into small staves of wood cut from the branch of a fruit bearing tree. I created mine from an apple tree. The rune letters themselves are sharp and angular, revealing their origins in the markings that blades can make in wood. Each of the rune letters is a symbol of some sacred power in the old German understanding of the universe.

Runes were used for magic, for divination, and for communicating with sacred forces. According to some German and Norse myths, the runes were given to the *God Odin*, after he hung suspended for nine days and nine nights on *Yggdrasil*, the sacred tree of the world. *Odin* then shared the runes with humankind. The runes were a gift from a holy tree.

Two of the runes are specifically linked to trees. *Eiwaz* represents the yew tree and *Berkana*, the birch tree. The yew tree is a symbol for Yggdrasil and is linked to death and the realm beyond death. The tree is poisonous and its wood was used to make long bows for hunting and war; and yet it lives to be perhaps the oldest tree we know. There is a yew tree called the Fortingall yew, which is situated in a churchyard in Perthshire, Scotland. It is believed to be the most ancient tree in Europe, between two and five thousand years old.

The birch tree, on the other hand, is linked to birth and beginnings. It is one of the first trees to grow in an area after a fire has destroyed its vegetation. Birch branches were used in cheerful springtime rituals, a symbol of new life and the fruitfulness of spring. When Margy and I were looking for a home in Maine, we were feeling discouraged after May and June had passed without our finding anything. We did a reading of the runes, and pulled out *Berkana*—the birch tree rune. It could be read as a great indicator of prosperous new beginnings coming into our life. But we also decided to take it more literally.

We began to look for houses that had anything to do with birch trees. We noticed an ad for a house on Birchwood Road, and saw another house described as having birch cabinets, and a few others like that. So we came up the last weekend in July to check them out, and then found another house in the newspaper on the last day. The backyard turned out to be full of birch trees. It was also exactly what we were looking for.

Some people believe the runes communicated magic messages. The rune alphabet encompassed a vocabulary of secret symbols that were understood by the spiritual leaders. But what strikes me most powerfully about the runes is the magic of writing and reading itself. This runic alphabet enabled the written transmission of words and ideas. What an uncanny ability it must have seemed at first—to communicate across distance or time in a way talking couldn't match.

The root of the word "rune" implies secret or hidden. A message could be carved out by one who knew the runes, and—sent via a messenger who did not know the message—it could be understood by another person far away. The ability of rune readers to communicate in silence with each other would have appeared magical to anyone who witnessed it. These messages could even endure beyond the death of their creators, to be received by those who came after. We have forgotten to be in awe of the power of that literacy.

Many years after I moved far away from the beech tree, I discovered another link. According to entomologist Gilbert Waldbauer, the ancient Germanic peoples would carve their runes on thin slabs of beech wood. These were sometimes laced together with leather strips to create what they called a *Buch*, which was the German word for both *beech* and *book*.[91] This tree was their original text, the bearer of all text. When I sat in the beech tree, I was face to face with that perennial yearning of humankind to leave our mark. I too had a yearning to leave my mark on paper, writing my thoughts and feelings, my hopes and memories, creating something new with the magic of words.

I started to write a journal when I was a young adult. It was 1979, and I was a year into my first serious relationship with a partner. Gary and I were deeply in love. But the first pages of an orange spiral notebook are filled with my confusion and pain about the struggles in our relationship. When things were difficult, he withdrew from me, and so I wrote about the pain I felt when he withdrew. I wrote about who we were together, and parts of myself that seemed to be disappearing. Perhaps I should thank him now—if he were a more consistent listener, maybe I wouldn't have started writing so much.

But once I started, writing became an important way of learning about myself, a spiritual practice that has continued to this day. I wrote my questions about how to live in the world, what my own calling might be, what brought me joy and what left me empty. I wrote my questions about *God*. It was in the same year, 1979, that I was wrestling with big questions of spirit and faith. I was introduced to the idea of the *Goddess*, and feminist women's spiritual circles. I wrote to *God*, to *Goddess*, to Jesus, all my questions and doubts— Are you real? Are you there for me? What am I meant to do in this life?

Writing is one more way to unburden our hearts and minds. We can take our weary feelings, our anger, our confusion, our loneliness, and we can put it outside of us, setting it down on paper. It can help us to let go, and move on. Writing can also take us more deeply into our own hearts and minds, and open us, layer upon layer, until we reach the place of inner wisdom. Polly Berends, author of *Coming to Life*, says, "Everything that happens to you is your teacher. The secret is to learn to sit at the feet of your own life and be taught by it."[92] Writing is a way of sitting at the feet of our own life and being taught by it.

A few years into my journaling, I began to mark the pages according to the cycles of the moon. Each new moon day, I began to read back to the last new moon, and sometimes I would give a theme to that moon time, like a chapter to a book: the traveling moon, the moon of discernment, the moon of confusion. To read through our own journal entries is another way of being taught by our lives.

Another tool has been to write to someone I care about—not to be sent to that person, but to express what I need to express to them. This can be especially powerful when we have lost someone we love to death. Gary and I were together for six years. After we had been separated for a few years, he was killed in an auto accident. I still loved him, and my heart felt broken at his passing. There was much left unfinished in our connection. I found I could write to him in my journal—I could tell him all the things that had been left unsaid between us. It was a way to find healing and bring closure to our relationship.

Another side to this writing is to write in the voice of the other person or being. Here is an example of what I mean. I ask a question, whatever question is deep in my heart. One of my perennial questions has been, "How can I learn to live in harmony with the earth?" I write it down. Then I let the voice of the trees answer the question. I do this literally. I write, "The trees say:" and then keep writing. Here is what came out when I asked this question most recently: "The trees say slow down, stop running everywhere, feel the wind on your face, feel the sun on your skin. Don't be afraid, you can do this. You belong to the earth."

It doesn't have to be trees. It could be the birds, the ocean, the moon. It could be myself at the age of eight. It could be my old love Gary. On a psychological level, in all of these exercises, what I am doing is tapping into parts of myself that hold wisdom. On a spiritual level, we are not separate from trees, birds, the ocean or the moon—so who is to say if we open our souls we can't hear the wisdom they might have for us? Writing connects us to the depths of our own hearts, and our hearts connect us to all that is.

Anne LeClaire, a writer I met while living on Cape Cod, says we must take up our pen "like a heat-seeking missile... aiming it for the territory of truth." We must go to the places we are afraid to go. We so often try to keep our hearts hidden, afraid to expose our secret selves. But LeClaire challenges us: "The heart of the universe is always within our own hearts if only we can be brave enough to expose it."[93]

Writing is a journey we take to discover who we are and what is true. Writing will surprise us. We don't know ahead of time what will come out on the page, what will emerge within our souls. Like the magic of the ancient runes carved in trees, writing reveals secrets to us. When I write in my journal, I do it on paper, and what is paper but very thin pressings made from wood? Each time I write, I enter this old partnership of human and tree. We join together to create a magic of exploration and memory which neither of us could do alone.

Trees have been the foundation of so much human life and culture. The first fuel of many of our ancestors was wood. Our houses are made of wood. The floors, the walls, the ceilings, the window frames and doorways. We are surrounded and held up and sheltered by the gifts of trees. Our musical instruments, our tools, our boats, many of our foods and medicines, all are possible because of trees. No wonder we say "Knock on wood" when everything is going well and we wish to protect ourselves from bad luck.

Trees also play a significant role in the crisis we face today for the health of our planet. Deforestation has contributed to global warming, and planting new trees can contribute to reducing the levels of carbon in the atmosphere. I am inspired by the work of the Green Belt Movement in Kenya, founded by Nobel Prize winner, Wangari Maathai. Beginning in 1977, Maathai responded to the needs of rural Kenyan women who told her their streams were going dry, their food supply was insecure, and they had to walk further and further to get firewood. She organized the women to grow seedlings and plant trees.

In this way they would restore damaged watersheds, and ensure future food and firewood.[94] Over fifty-one million trees have been planted in Kenya since they began.

I wish we Americans could go back to the old European pagan approach to trees. They didn't believe it was wrong to cut down trees or use their products for their needs. But the old pagans taught that before cutting a tree one must ask permission of the tree. To request its consent acknowledges we have a relationship of mutuality and respect. Some might say asking permission wouldn't alter the act of cutting the tree. But think about how consent and respect differentiate acts of lovemaking from acts of assault.

To relate to a tree with respect will change the nature of the use we make of it for our survival needs. I believe a tree is not merely a tool and resource for human needs. The tree is a sacred Other, with its own inherent value and meaning. How do we know the tree does not have its own sentient life? My lack of knowledge about its language does not determine the tree is without a language of its own. Recently, I learned trees emit low-frequency vibrations that human ears cannot detect.

There was one more communication I experienced with the four directions tree which was not about writing or speaking or even thinking. Sometimes I merely sat, my body balanced between the sturdiness of the main branches, my eyes resting on the translucent green leaves softening the sunlight. Even then, the tree and I were involved in a sacred exchange. When I breathed, the tree was my intimate partner. The tree breathed out the oxygen I needed to be alive, and I breathed out the carbon dioxide it used for nourishment. Our physical bodies are designed to need each other. We give and receive the very substance of our lives. We have been giving and receiving this way for millennia.

We and the trees are neighbors on this planet, but more than that, we are sacred partners, we are kin. We are genetically and spiritually related to each other. If we are open to respecting the trees, if we value the inherent dignity of the trees, it then becomes possible for us to experience in the trees the presence of the *Divine Mystery*.

Breathing and writing, dreaming and remembering, in the sacred arms of the beech tree, I tasted what it felt like to be held by *God* and to be one with *God*. I tasted what it felt like to be held by the earth. The trees teach us that all of us are related; their quiet language sings the song of the marvelous interweaving unity of life on earth. Remember this, the next time you walk by the trees near where you live. Listen. And then remember to say thanks.

PRACTICE

Get an inexpensive notebook
and begin writing your thoughts and feelings.
If you have a tree you can visit,
write while sitting under the tree.
You don't have to write every day.
But make time for it at least once a week.
When you have an important question, write it down.
Then imagine a response from another being's perspective,
perhaps a tree.
On the day of the new moon,
read over what you have written during the past month.
Notice if there are themes or insights or wisdom
you have gleaned from your life,
and write those down for that day's entry.
Pick a theme for that month.

17: A Bowl Full of the Universe

I believe it was Laguna Pueblo author, Paula Gunn Allen, who said it, but now I can't find the original quote. It went something like this: "Many people think of consciousness as an attribute of being human, but we know that consciousness is an attribute of being."

I have been intrigued and transformed by her observation. What might it mean that human beings are not alone in perceiving, in awareness, in communication? Sometimes the scientists ask those questions about beings most like humans—apes, dolphins, dogs. But beyond that? And not even merely beings with eyes as we know them? I wonder about it. Trees are sensitive to light and plants turn toward the sun. Isn't it less lonely to imagine trees, birds, water, and stones are conscious, too?

Our culture has wanted to feel human beings are unique. That we are above the rest of the created world, special. Even in our growing ecological understanding there is a sense we are the privileged children of the universe. I have heard many ecologists express the sentiment that we are the universe becoming conscious of itself, drawing from astronomer Carl Sagan's statement, "We are a way for the cosmos to know itself." And it is a tremendous gift that we are able to perceive and explore and study the universe of which we are a part. But how do we know we are the only conscious ones? How dare we assume we are the only ones? Why would we want to be the only ones?

In the congregation in which I serve as minister, we have an auction every other year. One of the items auctioned off is a chance to request a sermon topic. One year the member who won requested I talk about nuclear weapons. Well, sure, I said… and then I put the suggestion in my sermon topic folder. Each month as I chose themes for the next month's services, I would see it there, but I wasn't sure yet what I would do with it. What could I say about nuclear weapons?

I was reminded of the old story about President Calvin Coolidge. One Sunday, with his wife sick, he went to church alone. Upon his return she asked, "What did the pastor talk about?" Coolidge said, "Sin." "And what did the minister say about sin?" "He was against it." Well that's about what I had for nuclear weapons: I was against them.

How do we face the biggest dangers that threaten our world? For me, a worship service should be about hope. And nuclear weapons feel terrifying. The mushroom-cloud image of the atomic bomb represents the potential destruction of most life on earth. I didn't feel like researching how bad things were, what new weapons were being created, or who might try to use them. And most of all, I wasn't sure what I could say next. I never want to send people home from worship with more fear or despair than they came in with. So the topic sat in my folder, and I occasionally added an article or resource to the file; but each month, I'd say, I'll do that one another time.

Several months later, I came upon an article that gave me new courage for dealing with the nuclear topic. It was about mushrooms, of all things, an interview with Paul Stamets, author of *Mycelium Running: How Mushrooms Can Help Save the World.*[95] I have to admit I previously had not been a big fan of mushrooms. I tolerated their presence on pizza and in casserole dishes. I had never experimented with the psychedelic varieties back in college. A while ago, Margy started taking photos of mushrooms as they popped up in our back yard, and that helped me to appreciate their strange and diverse beauty. But I had no idea about their other remarkable properties.

I learned mushrooms were the fruit of the mycelium, a vast underground network of fungal fibers that can stretch for miles. Those fibers form one entity called a mycelial mat. A mycelial mat in eastern Oregon was considered by scientists to be the largest organism in the world. It covers twenty-two hundred acres and is more than two thousand years old.

Mycelial networks regulate the nutrients of plant life in the forest, transferring sugars from trees that have enough to other tree species that need more to survive. And most astonishing of all, mycelial networks communicate. To do this they use methods similar to those found in the nerve fibers in our own brains; they use some of the very same neurotransmitters that allow us to think.

Stamets, referring back to the Gaia hypothesis, says:

> I see mycelium as the living network that manifests the natural intelligence imagined by Gaia theorists. The mycelium is an exposed sentient membrane, aware and responsive to changes in its environment. As hikers, deer or insects walk across these sensitive filamentous nets, they leave impressions, and mycelia sense and respond to these movements. A complex and resourceful structure for sharing information, mycelium can adapt and evolve through the ever-changing forces of nature.[96]

In other words, he proposes there is a vast, intelligent, and aware network in the ground beneath our feet. It causes me to wonder, what is intelligence? Human beings consider ourselves to be the most intelligent species on earth. Our intelligence has given us the power to build nuclear weapons that can destroy life on earth. But we haven't yet been able to figure out how to avoid war and environmental destruction.

Stamets believes the mycelium operates at a level of complexity that exceeds the computational powers of our most advanced supercomputers. He sees the mycelium as the earth's natural Internet. Traditional Mexican shamans and *curanderas* use certain mushrooms that create visions and healing. Stamets says psychoactive mushrooms can cause such effects on the human mind because of the chemicals we share in common.

On a practical level, it has been discovered that mycelial mats have the capacity to break down petroleum products into harmless components; they can also clean up nerve gas agents, dioxin, plastics, and radioactive cesium. Stamets believes mycelia not only have "the ability to protect the environment but the intelligence to do it on purpose."[97]

Mycelial networks are a visceral manifestation of the interconnected web of life, and we can see and measure their beneficial support for plant life, and for our lives. Scientists like Stamets imagine if we partner with mycelia, we would be able to greatly accelerate our work to repair the damage we have done to our environment. And that gives me hope for our future.

With these mysterious mycelial allies beneath my feet, I had the courage to write that sermon about nuclear weapons, and their haunting mushroom clouds of death. It became a sermon as much about mushrooms and their astounding powers of life. Each time I remember this old and vast elemental wisdom, I feel less fear. I feel more clearly that I am only one small part of a larger network of beings who are contributing to the health and wholeness of the planet. As we reach out to the beautiful web of all beings, those beings are also reaching out to us.

There are helpers and elders all around us, there is wisdom, if we open to it. There are animals and plants and fungal networks, and rivers and mountains and the wild winds. We can enter into relationship with all beings, and find help from them for the great struggles of our time. We have not been looking to our relatives and our ancestors for connection, and so we often are unaware of the powers that exist all around us. When Paula Gunn Allen speaks of consciousness as an attribute of being, it helps me to move beyond the narrow vision of my own culture, and claim my own experience of relationship with other beings.

Once, after the difficult ending to a relationship, I was rocking in a hammock on the back porch of the home I would soon have to leave. In that place of loneliness and unknown futures, I saw something like an image, felt a presence. Later I described it in a poem:

How can I trust my senses
in a moment full of loneliness
when the old dark woman appears
gray hair gathered in a bun in the back

squatting near a fire holding
a bowl full of the universe?[98]

It is an ancient Innu grandmother, my ancient Innu grandmother from many generations ago, and in her hands she is holding a bowl. I can see darkness and stars swirling inside. Even though the container she holds is small, humble, it opens up to so much more—the entire universe is there, the oneness of everything, the larger whole of which we are a part, infinity. The Innu grandmother says to me, "The universe is in your heart, and you are in the heart of the universe."

There are beings all around us who want to be called upon, who want to help us in this work of returning to wholeness, this work of finding our way home. I have shared stories of a few of the beings who have helped me. The chamomile plant who calms anxiety. The bright red cardinal singing its beautiful song. The four directions beech tree. The waters of lakes and streams and the ocean. The ground, the very ground we walk upon, that holds me when all around me everything is falling apart.

Now that I know about the mycelial network, the ground feels more alive to me. But it was always true that something happened when I sat down upon the ground. If I sleep on the ground for a longer period of days, there is a glow that surrounds my body. I remember this from my time at the Women's Peace Camp, where I was sleeping in a tent for months. I felt alive in some new way I began to miss when I went back inside an apartment in Chicago. I forget it easily, but I feel more alive when I am outside.

Just as we can now sit in front of a plastic and metal panel and communicate with people across the world, so there are technologies to communicate across species and across dimensions. The threads of life weave us together in ways we have barely begun to imagine. But I know this: we belong here together and we need each other now more than ever. Poet Barbara Deming writes,

Our own pulse beats in every stranger's throat,
And also there within the flowered ground beneath our feet,

And—teach us to listen!—
We can hear it in water, in wood, and even in stone.
We are earth of this earth, and we are bone of its bone.
This is a prayer I sing...[99]

Because we are all connected, any small action we take has the capacity to affect the wider network. When we begin to honor and celebrate our connection with even one other being on this planet, something reverberates through the whole web. When we express our gratitude for the water we drink, and do our part to preserve its cleanliness, we are nurturing the web of life. When we listen, really listen to the water, the wood, and the stone, we are nurturing the web of life.

We are not alone. In this time of great challenges and transitions, there are a host of beings who love life and who want to help us find another way to live. As we reach out to them, they are reaching out to us.

PRACTICE

Go outside carrying a journal and pen.
Walk around slowly for about five minutes.
Observe, smell, listen, touch.
As you walk, find one living being to give deeper attention
—a plant, a tree, a stone, a bee, a mushroom—
whatever being sparks your interest.
Stay with that being quietly for five minutes.
Try to imagine what the world is like
from the perspective of that being.
Offer thanks to the being for its part in the circle of life.
Then, after five minutes are over,
imagine the being has a message for you.
Write it down in the voice of the being
to which you are paying attention.
Feel free to ask questions
and hear what the answers might be.
When you finish, offer thanks again.
Make it a practice to visit that same being regularly if you can.

*Learn more about the animals and plants
in the place where you live.*

18: Come Dance

Just hours after the earthquake had devastated their city, the people of Port-au-Prince were marching and singing and dancing through the rubble-filled streets, clapping their hands. As night fell, and a deep darkness with no electricity enveloped the ruins, everyone was outside. Families slept in makeshift tents, in fear of aftershocks, but also in solidarity, and they continued singing through the night. One person commented to a reporter that it was an expression of community. In the face of tragedy and survival, song and dance and prayer carried the people through that long night before any help arrived.

One November several years ago, I traveled to Ottawa, Ontario for a convocation of ministers. It was a great time for connecting with colleagues, but for me it also became a time for connecting with my ancestors. My mother's mother and father had met each other in Ottawa, sometime soon after 1912. His name was Johann, and he had come to Canada with a small group of buddies from Austria, via France and England, all of them working as waiters during their travels. He got a job as a waiter at the Chateau Laurier—a brand new luxury hotel in the heart of the nation's capital, the spot where the movers and shakers gathered to make deals and lead the country. My grandmother Yvonne began working as a chambermaid in the same hotel. She had been living in the suburban Quebec village of Hull.

Our conference in Ottawa was around the corner from the Chateau Laurier. I visited there several times, finding the original dining room where my grandfather might have served tables, and the back stairwell the maids would have used as they went from floor to floor cleaning the rooms. I wondered what it must have been like, to be surrounded by luxury, and yet working in the humblest of jobs. I don't know how they met and fell in love, but in 1915 they traveled to Detroit, Michigan where they married and raised a family.

I was also curious about what I might learn about my great-grandmother Claudia, whose name was given to me as my middle name. The one picture I have of her shows a tired-looking woman in a simple worn dress. I imagined she had had a hard life. She was born on a farm near Lac-St-Jean, Quebec but had traveled far away from home with her husband, Ferdinand, who was listed as a laborer in the census. They survived the great fire that burned down a good portion of the town of Hull, and traveled to South Dakota with their children so Ferdinand could work in the mica mines for five years. In her older age, Claudia lived in the Ottawa area, but I don't know what happened to Ferdinand.

I wanted to find her gravesite, but didn't even know the date of her death or the cemetery where she was buried. By some Internet searching, and a minor miracle, I received an email shortly after I arrived in Ottawa with the information I needed. Each time I have traveled to Quebec, it seems my ancestors have reached out to me in some way. This was one of those times. One afternoon, I took a bus out to the Notre Dame Cemetery and found Claudia's small headstone. It was all by itself—no other family members were buried nearby—which seemed lonely. I sat by her grave and imagined the life she must have led, imagined the burdens she must have carried. I expect that many of my ancestors led hard lives; they struggled to feed their families and to give their children a chance.

Later, back at the conference, we were treated to a concert that concluded with the group, Genticorum, who played and sang traditional French Canadian music. It was lively and fun and pulled many of us out of our seats to dance in the aisles. The songs were in French, but the singer would introduce them by telling us the topic. The lyrics of one song turned out to be the recipe for pea soup, a traditional Quebecois food. There were a few other songs about food too.

Suddenly I realized my perceptions of my ancestors' lives had been not quite accurate. Yes, the winters were long and perilous, and farmers had to grow enough food to live on, and there were probably times when supplies were stretched pretty thin. Yes, there were fires and migrations and hard labor. Margaret Atwood says the great theme of Canadian literature is survival.[100] But what do people do when they're hungry and trying to survive? They sing about food. They sing and they dance and that gives them the energy to keep on going.

And I remembered again something my mother had said about my grandmother Yvonne. She loved to go out dancing, all throughout her life. It opened up the possibility of a very different picture of my great-grandmother Claudia—perhaps she, too, had been a woman who danced. Dancing was a strategy for surviving hard times, as well as enjoying good times.

Worship in my own culture usually includes beautiful music and a lot of words, but not much movement. We leave our bodies out of the process. But our bodies and spirits are designed for movement. In the beginning, there was no separation between music and dance. We don't know whether music evolved before or after language, but we do know early human beings sang and danced. It was central to their worship, their healing, their community bonds, their rituals. Dance was a part of the festivals and gatherings of people around the world. Dance was a way to praise the *Divine*, and to enter into the very essence of *being*, losing oneself in the great joy. Daniel Ladinsky writes, interpreting the Sufi poet Hafiz, about "the God who only knows four words... 'Come dance with Me.'" [101]

All around us there is evidence the universe is in constant movement, a cosmic fractal dance. The earth spins around its axis each day and night, planets spin around the sun, the stars spin in galaxies. We know tiny atoms, too, are full of the invisible vibrations of subatomic particles. The natural world is made of intricate rhythms and orderly patterns of movement. When we dance, perhaps we, too, are part of the vast dance of the sun, the earth, the moon, the stars.

Once, years ago, I created a moon calendar for a young friend who was six years old at the time. I was curious myself about why the moon was sometimes seen in the morning, and sometimes in the evening, and it changed every day. I thought it would be fun to learn about it and share it with her. So I tracked it, and began to understand its cycles.

The moon is always half in light and half in darkness from the light of the sun. When the moon is full, we are seeing the whole of its light side, because the sun and moon are on opposite sides of our sky. The full moon rises at sunset and stays in the sky all night, setting at sunrise. Then, as the days go by, we see less of the light of the moon and more of its shadow, and it rises about fifty minutes later each day, until there is only a waning crescent in the morning just before and after dawn. About two weeks after the full moon, the moon rises unseen with the sun and sets invisibly with the sun. The night is dark. This is called the dark moon or the new moon. Then a day or two later, a thin waxing crescent appears in the western sky just after sunset and sets soon after. Each day it is seen in the evening for a little longer time until we come round to full moon again.

The tides of the sea are dancing along with the rhythm of the moon. One of Margy's and my friends didn't understand about tides. We were planning to go swimming with her on a Wednesday at the beach where we can only swim near high tide. Two days before, she was visiting the beach and called us from there to make plans. "The sign at the beach house says high tide is at 2 p.m.," she said, "Shall we meet at 2 on Wednesday?" We had to explain to her the tide would be later in two days, closer to 3:40 p.m.; that it changes every day.

The stars also form a pattern to our eyes in the night sky. They circle around the North Star, so when people take a time-lapse photo, you see the stars as lines in circles around that point. Of course, it is really the earth that is moving, revolving on its axis pointing toward Polaris. Every revolving planet will have its own North Star.

The ancients used to tell time by the stars. If you were to track the Big Dipper, you could watch it move around the sky during the night, and if you watched it over many weeks, you'd see it was in a different place in the circle, each month of the year. Our ancestors were watching all these patterns, learning them and remembering them so they might tell their children, marking them so we would know how to plant and harvest and hunt, and dance our own dance of time.

One time in late winter I began to trudge along through my days, feeling burdened by my activities, and forgetting to notice the beauty of life or feel the joy of life. When I was in a moment of quiet time, my spirit told me I needed to dance. I remembered that when I was in the women's spirituality group many years ago, our rituals always included a time of free-form dance. When we climbed up to Blueberry Hill, we would light a fire, and then chant together and dance around the circle. During those hours, I felt at home in the universe, connected to all of life.

So when my spirit told me I needed to dance, it wasn't a brand new idea. But I hadn't had the opportunity to celebrate like that in a long time. Cross-cultural anthropologist Angeles Arrien says in many traditional cultures, when ill persons go to the healer, one of the questions they are asked is "When did you stop dancing?"[102]

I knew dance could be a powerful form of prayer. So how could I bring it back into my life? First of all, I looked online to see what might be out there for dancing. I found some groups doing ecstatic dance, an authentic and free-form style of dance. That sounded great, but I didn't find any programs that fit my complicated schedule right away. Then I thought—just do it! I listen to the radio in my car, and I notice songs that speak to me in some way, and lately there had been several that also had a rhythm inviting movement. I believe we can find spiritual inspiration almost anywhere, so why not use what was right there in front of me?

I downloaded several songs, put them on a dance playlist, and then started taking dance breaks during the day. I stop my work, put on my earphones, and dance enthusiastically to one song. Amazingly, after that three- or four-minute dance break, I feel energized and happy. It isn't logical, it is physical. Sometimes it feels almost miraculous. *Balter* is an old English word meaning to dance gracelessly, without particular art or skill, but perhaps with some enjoyment. I am engaging in the spiritual practice of baltering.

How could something so simple be so powerful? I am not super fit, but I could move around for a few minutes. Experts now say doing exercise in short bursts is beneficial for your heart and your health. And there is something about music that gives energy for movement. I remember during my time at the Women's Peace Camp, we might end the day exhausted, but then start singing songs around the campfire, and be revitalized. About once a week, we put on recorded music and had a "wild dance party."

There is something about dancing and singing that brings us out of our left brain and into our right brain. It brings us out of doing and into being. It brings us out of our small selves and into a reality larger than our troubles. My ancestors had gotten it right. And especially during these times when what is going on around us seems overwhelming, don't we need to find more ways to connect with what is larger than ourselves? How can we be at home in a dancing universe without being a part of the dance?

There is an old story about a famous rabbi who came to a small Russian village. The people began to prepare for his visit with great anticipation, and gathered the questions they wanted to ask this wise and revered teacher. When the rabbi arrived, they all met in the town square, and began to clamor for his attention, expressing all their struggles and questions about life. The rabbi felt their tension and their expectations, and was quiet for a long while, closing his eyes. The crowd got quiet too. He began to softly hum a little tune and sway from side to side. Presently, the people began to find themselves humming and swaying with him.

Then the rabbi began to dance, slowly at first, but soon faster and faster, and all the villagers joined in, until the square was full of dancing and singing. Hours passed before the dance was done, and then the people were sitting in the square, tired and still. The rabbi looked at the group with tenderness and said, "I trust I have answered all your questions." And they went home that night with joyful hearts.

PRACTICE

Everyone's body has different capabilities and vulnerabilities,
so adapt this for your own body.
Put on some music and feel the rhythms.
Begin to move your hands and arms around.
Once that feels comfortable,
begin to sway your torso from side to side.
If you can, stand up and begin to move your feet around too.
Clap your hands if you feel like it, or stomp your feet.
Jump up and down if that works for you.
Take emotional risks, but honor your body's limits.
Move your body in whatever way the music is moving.
Dance to just one song, or a dozen.
Don't think about it, just move.
At the end, be still.
Stillness is also a part of the dance.

19: I See the Mountain

I saw a cartoon the other day. Four people were sitting in a boat that had tilted precariously and was filling with water at one end. The two people at that end were bailing furiously. The two people at the other end were sitting high and dry—and one said to the other, "It's good that our end of the boat isn't leaking."

We are all in the same boat—this planet earth. The only real future we can create is a common future. When we finally realize we are one family, one interconnected whole, essentially united with each other and with the earth, we will be able to find a way forward together. I believe we are already on the path.

We are living in a time of transformation. Ecologist Joanna Macy calls it *The Great Turning.*[103] We are trying to shift from an industrial-growth society to a life-sustaining earth community. A part of that turning is a transformation of our understanding and practice of spirituality. We need to find our way home to our spiritual interconnection. We belong to earth, to each other and to the great *Mysteries* that move within and between us. We need to wake up to that belonging. If we love the earth, we can find a way live ecologically. If we recognize all people are one family, we can sort out how to care for each other in these times. If we call for help from our kindred beings in the natural and spiritual world, we can find hope.

Change is already happening. There are millions of people and groups who are in some way involved in this new vision of earth community, and we can be a part of it. Co-founder of the Positive Futures Network, David Korten, calls our attention to the familiar story of the caterpillar and butterfly. We all know the story. The caterpillar spends its days gorging itself on nature's bounty. Then it attaches to a twig and forms a chrysalis around itself in order to become a butterfly. What we might not know is what's happening inside the chrysalis to shape the butterfly.

Korten, drawing on the work of evolution biologists, writes:

> ...the structures of its cellular tissue begin to dissolve into an organic soup.
>
> Yet, guided by some deep inner wisdom, a number of *organizer cells* begin to rush around gathering others cells to form *imaginal buds*, initially independent multicellular structures that begin to give form to the organs of a new creature. Correctly perceiving a threat to the old order, but misdiagnosing the source, the caterpillar's still intact immune system attributes the threat to the imaginal buds and attacks them as alien intruders.
>
> The imaginal buds prevail by linking up with one another in a cooperative effort that brings forth a new being of great beauty, wondrous possibilities, and little identifiable resemblance to its progenitor.[104]

Korten sees our cultural transformation in a similar vein. Individuals wake up from the prevailing social systems and perspectives, and begin to align our lives with the values of partnership and earth community. At first we experience a sense of isolation, but eventually we find others who share those values, and form what educator Parker Palmer calls "communities of congruence."[105] Those small beginnings attract others—we are like the imaginal buds of the new culture.

The old culture perceives us as a threat and often attacks our work. But as we network with others who share in the new cultural values, change begins to happen. Korten believes the cultural transformation we need is already in process—we can see the evidence of its beginnings in the great social-change movements of the last half of the twentieth century—for civil rights, women's equality, peace, environmental balance, and economic justice.[106]

Martin Luther King, Jr., in his last speech given in Memphis on the day before he died, says, "We've got some difficult days ahead. But it doesn't matter with me now. Because I've been to the mountaintop. …I've seen the promised land."[107] I used to think this meant that in some mysterious way he had seen the future, and he had faith that black people would eventually win their rights.

But I saw it differently after I was involved in the struggle for equal marriage for same-sex couples in Massachusetts. I now believe the mountaintop is less about a prophecy of the future, and more about an experience in the present. Two members of my congregation on Cape Cod were plaintiffs in the lawsuit for equal marriage. They told me how terrifying it was, in the days leading up to the lawsuit, to ask the town clerk for a marriage license when they knew the answer would be no. It was scary to be publicly identified as lesbians and to speak to news reporters. It was also frightening for many couples who had hidden their relationships to have a conversation with their legislator or their neighbor, or to carry a sign in public.

But each new act in honor of their love lessened their fear and strengthened their dignity. Same-sex couples became aware of the burden they had been carrying, the hidden assumption they were somehow less than the others. Once they had felt a glimpse of equality, they couldn't go back. They had put down the burden, and they were free, and every one of us felt the joy spreading over our community. So, even if opponents standing outside the Massachusetts State House were holding signs that said, "Homosexuals are demons," it didn't matter. I saw a young lesbian woman carrying another poster that said, "Your signs are mean but we love you anyway." No matter what happened next, our shared vision released an inner power that was indestructible.

I think that is what Dr. King was talking about. He knew there was something bigger than oppression, something stronger than those who might kill him. It was visceral and immediate. By joining with others to tap the power of love and equality through non-violent action, he felt first-hand a new way of being in the world. He fully experienced his own dignity and the dignity of his people. After that, what else could matter? He had been to the mountaintop. As he says, "whenever men and women straighten their backs up, they are going somewhere..."[108] He knew there was no turning back.

The mountain has been a spiritual symbol across many cultures and times. The highest mountains were not places people could live, so they became places to go away from daily life, and into another consciousness. They represent wilderness and mystery. Prophets and mystics went into the mountains to find *God*. Some Native American traditions teach that mountains are the home of the *Spirits*. Dr. King was quoting the story of Moses, who was taken up to the mountaintop to view the land promised to his people, even though he would not live to enter it with them.

The mountain is a challenge. It is difficult to climb to the top. It reminds us of how small we are. It makes us humble. The mountain is a symbol of the ability to perceive the long view. On the top of the mountain we can see for miles all around us. We can see where we are and where we are going. Before the days of airplanes and rockets, the mountaintop was the only place where we could notice the unity of the earth. We could see the distant waters of the ocean, and the hills and valleys in between, the farms and forests, the roads and houses. We could see the meandering paths of the rivers, all flowing toward the sea.

Even viewing the mountain from below helps us in many ways. When we are journeying in the valleys and foothills, we can look up to the mountain, and use it to orient ourselves, to guide our path. We say, oh, there is the mountain to my left, or to my right; now I know where I am, now I can find my way. The mountain represents vision and clarity, whether we are looking out from the mountaintop, or looking up at the mountain. For me, the mountain is what is most real and solid, what can be relied upon. It is something bigger than any troubles. It symbolizes my hope for the world.

Once we catch sight of a new way of being, we are forever changed. We start to live differently. Even if the society around us is slow to change. Even when the enormity of the task before us feels so much bigger than we are. And there are times when I do feel overwhelmed by the destruction going on every day. Tar sands oil, fracking for natural gas, extinction of species, clear cutting of forests, climate change, poverty and greed, hate and war. There are times when all the work we do doesn't seem to make a dent in the problems.

I found hope in a mountain story I was told by a woman from one of my former congregations. An American, she had married a man whose family was from India. While they were traveling in India with their small baby, she heard many people talk about the beauty and majesty of the Himalayan Mountains. Finally, they got a chance to visit Darjeeling, a hill station in the foothills of the Himalayas. Mark Twain says of Darjeeling, it is "the one land that all men desire to see, and having seen once, by even a glimpse, would not give that glimpse for the shows of all the rest of the globe combined."[109]

However, when they arrived in Darjeeling, it was cloudy and rainy, and their accommodations were cramped and dirty. After a couple days of this, the baby was fussing and cranky and the woman found herself exhausted and irritated in the midst of what was supposed to have been the highlight of their travels. Then, one day, while she was feeling utterly down in the dumps, sitting on the little balcony outside their room, the clouds broke, the sun shone through, and there was the mountain, *Kanchenjunga*, the King of the Mountains, vast, huge, and unimaginably powerful, like nothing she had ever seen before.

After a few minutes, the clouds covered over again. She did not see the mountain again during the rest of their stay. But that was fine. One glimpse had been enough. Everywhere she went in the town, she felt its nearness, its power, its mystery, even though all she could see now was rain and clouds.[110]

Once we catch sight of a new way of being, we are forever changed. Once we glimpse the *Divine Mystery*, we cannot forget it. Once we wake up to our connection to the earth community, we cannot go back to sleep. We are on a long journey, but we do not walk in confusion. The clouds may cover the mountain, *Kanchenjunga*, but they cannot destroy it or take it away. One glimpse is enough to establish its presence. We might go through an entire journey almost never seeing it. But it is there, and all we need is one glimpse to save us. As folk musician poet Dave Carter sang, "I see the mountain, and that is all I see."[111]

I am remembering back to the ritual I shared with the other women on Blueberry Hill, when the night turned foggy and we couldn't see anything around us. We had a moment of panic. It seemed as if we were on a small island, and the rest of the world had disappeared. But we knew the way home, even if we couldn't see the path. Our feet found the path down the hill.

"What is really going on?" we ask. Earth community. Breathing, dancing, diving into water, sitting in a tree, watching in the dark, changing our lives step by step, joining with others to change together. We don't know what the future will look like, but we sense the way through our feet, in the fog of today. The future is present in the *Mystery Seed* within us. We hear it in the songs of the cardinals. We are helping to create it by our magic and our transformations. We are calling for help from all the beautiful beings around us. So we live in a paradox. We are on a long journey, but we know the way home. And even in the midst of the journey, we are already there. We have been to the mountaintop. Wendell Berry writes,

"And the world cannot be discovered by a journey of miles, no matter how long, but only by a spiritual journey, a journey of one inch, very arduous and humbling and joyful, by which we arrive at the ground at our feet, and learn to be at home."[112]

Acknowledgements

I want to thank my partner in love and life, Margy Dowzer, who is the first reader (and sometimes editor) of every sermon I preach, as well as my companion on the journey into earth community. I have always trusted her good advice, and her encouragement enables me to send my words out into the world.

Special thanks also to the members and friends of my congregation, Allen Avenue Unitarian Universalist Church, who were the first audience for some of the stories and ideas that found their way into the book. I so appreciate our chance to learn about interconnection together.

I cannot imagine this book without the professional editing provided by Mark Chimsky. His enthusiastic support and detailed, on-target comments moved this project from its rough beginnings as a pile of sermons into a strong narrative to tell the story my heart desired to share. I will be forever grateful.

I also am grateful to friends and colleagues who read the manuscript during its various revisions, and provided encouragement and feedback along the way: Mary McCartney and Monique Chapman, for being the first ones to read the very early, much-longer draft, and for telling me they loved it. Deborah Cayer, for believing in the work and suggesting that I start blogging when I was discouraged after early publishing attempts. She opened a doorway for me into renewed creativity. For support and suggestions along the way, Virginia Marie Rincon, Marie Canaves, Lisa Greber, Estelle Coleman, gkisedtanamoogk, Ana Teresa Ortiz, Gail Geisenhainer, Denis Meacham, Kurt Kuhwald, Karen Brammer, Mike Freethy, and Heather Foran. Thanks to Carolyn Gage for introducing me to the liberating practice of self-publishing.

I love my mom and dad, Carol and Richard, whose deep faith started me on a spiritual path, and all my siblings who love me despite the differences in our perspectives. In telling my story, of course, some of their stories are intertwined with mine. I trust the reader to understand that these tellings are my own memories and interpretations, which may not be the same as the memories and interpretations of my family members.

I also honor the teachers and authors whose work has been pivotal to my journey: Amata Fabbro, Dorothy Day, Mary Daly, Audre Lorde, Paula Gunn Allen, Starhawk, Mab Segrest, Linda Hogan, and Joanna Macy.

Thank you to all the Catholic Workers, peace camp womyn, anti-racism activists, permaculture gardeners, UU ministers, and dreamers of the Great Turning with whom I have imagined new ways of being in the world.

And in particular, finally, I thank the non-human teachers named or unnamed in the pages of this book, and the ancestors who have come to my aid. May it be a blessing.

About the Author

Minister and earth activist, Myke Johnson currently serves the Allen Avenue Unitarian Universalist Church in Portland, Maine, while practicing and teaching ecological spirituality. Her ongoing writing is posted at findingourwayhome.blog.

She earned a Master of Divinity from Chicago Theological Seminary in 1986 and a Doctor of Ministry from Episcopal Divinity School in 1991. In 1993, *Women's Studies Quarterly* published an article based on her theological work, "Casting a New Circle: A Feminist Ritual Thealogy." Her writing has also appeared in *Christianity & Crisis, Sojourner, Sinister Wisdom, Trivia, At the Crossroads, Gay Community News, Lesbian Contradiction, The Brown Papers,* and *Quest.*

Prior to parish ministry, Myke was a psychotherapist and educator doing research, writing, teaching, and activism on lesbian/gay identity and liberation, anti-oppression organizing, disability access, Native sovereignty and land rights, and the intersection of spirituality and justice politics.

Beginning in 1992, she designed and led workshops for other white people on the problem of cultural appropriation of Native spirituality, through her organization RESPECT, Inc. (Responsible Ethics for Spirituality: Project to End Cultural Theft). In 1995, the Women's Theological Center in Boston published her essay, "Wanting to Be Indian: When Spiritual Searching Turns into Cultural Theft." It was then posted on Native websites and reposted around the world. In 2000, it appeared in *Pangaia Magazine,* and in 2001 was translated into German for the Swiss magazine, *Spuren.*

Working as an ally to Native peoples' political struggles opened her eyes to the importance of non-Indigenous people doing their own spiritual work to re-connect to the land, and was a catalyst to the personal journey which ultimately led to this book.

Last year, Myke and her life partner, Margy Dowzer, embarked on a search for greener housing. They moved into a smaller house with a big yard in Portland, and installed extra insulation, heat pumps and solar panels. They are now dreaming of planting a food forest in the back yard. In the meantime, you might find Myke singing a song, jumping in the Presumpscot River, playing with their two cats, Billie and Sassy, or taking a walk near the Capisic Brook at dawn.

Notes

[1] Allan Savory, *Holistic Management: A New Framework for Decision Making* (Washington, DC: Island Press, 1999), 20-21. I first learned of this story from Starhawk, *Earth Path, Grounding Your Spirit in the Rhythms of Nature* (New York: Harper Collins, 2004), 9.

[2] The term "earth community" evokes for me the interconnected web of all living beings on earth. It was used originally by the *Earth Charter* as an expression of a society built on partnership among people and with the natural world, with universal responsibility to and for one another and the earth. See http://earthcharter.org/discover/the-earth-charter/.

[3] Linda Hogan, *Dwellings: A Spiritual History of the Living World* (New York: W. W. Norton, 1995), 40.

[4] Christine Bochen, ed., *Thomas Merton: Essential Writings* (Maryknoll, NY: Orbis Books, 2000), 48.

[5] Leslie Marmon Silko, *The Turquoise Ledge: A Memoir* (New York: Viking, 2010).

[6] Mona Polacca is one of the Council of Thirteen Indigenous Grandmothers. See more at their webpage at http://www.grandmotherscouncil.org/who-we-are/grandmother-mona-polacca.

[7] Warren St. John and Alex Williams, "The Crow of the Early Bird," *The New York Times*, March 27, 2005, accessed at http://www.nytimes.com/2005/03/27/health/the-crow-of-the-early-bird.html.

[8] At Aquinas College in Grand Rapids, Michigan.

[9] Gal. 3:28 (*The New Oxford Annotated Bible*, 3rd Edition).

[10] Mary Daly, *Beyond God the Father* (Boston: Beacon Press, 1973).

[11] Ntozake Shange, the last line from her 1976 play, *For Colored Girls Who Have Considered Suicide/ When the Rainbow is Enuf*, (New York: Scribner, 1997).

[12] Henry David Thoreau, *Walden,* with introduction and annotations by Bill McKibben (Boston: Beacon Press, 1997, 1854), 249-250.

[13] Leslie Marmon Silko, *Yellow Woman and a Beauty of the Spirit* (New York: Simon & Schuster, 1996), 94.

[14] Dr. Jill Clapperton and Dr. Megan Ryan, "Uncovering the Real Dirt on No-Till" at http://www.sdnotill.com/Newsletters/Real%20Dirt.pdf.

[15] James Lovelock, *Gaia: A new look at life on Earth (Oxford University Press, 1979).*

[16] Barbara Kingsolver, with Steven L. Hopp and Camille Kingsolver, *Animal, Vegetable, Miracle: A Year of Food Life* (New York: HarperCollins, 2007).

[17] Ralph Waldo Emerson, "Introduction," *Nature: Addresses and Lectures* (1849).

[18] Breathing meditation adapted from Starhawk, *The Spiral Dance: A Rebirth of the Ancient Religion of the Great Goddess* (Harper & Row, San Francisco, 1979), 43.

[19] Karen Armstrong, *The Case for God* (New York: Alfred Knopf, 2009), xi.

[20] From a traditional Zen story, found in many places, including: http://www.awakeblogger.com/2008/11/the-meaning-of-the-finger-pointing-to-the-moon/.

[21] Kinrei Bassis, "The Buddha Calling the Buddha," *Parabola* 31 #2 (Summer 2006): 26.

[22] Coleman Barks, trans., *The Soul of Rumi: A New Collection of Ecstatic Poems* (SanFrancisco: Harper Collins, 2002), 77.

[23] Jack Kornfield, *After the Ecstasy, the Laundry: How the Heart Grows Wise on the Spiritual Path* (New York: Bantam, 2000), 126.

[24] Benoit Mandelbrot, *The Fractal Geometry of Nature* (New York: Times Books, 1982, 1977), 1.

[25] I didn't go into complex numbers or imaginary numbers, so my apologies to anyone who really knows about all of this. But for the rest of us, it is probably more than enough anyway. For those who want more detail, see *Introduction to the Mandelbrot Set: A guide for people with little math experience* by David Dewey, at: http://ddewey.net/mandelbrot/.

[26] *Hunting the Hidden Dimension,* Produced and Directed by Michael Schwarz and Bill Jersey, © 2008 WGBH Educational Foundation and The Catticus Corporation. For more information: http://www.pbs.org/wgbh/nova/physics/hunting-hidden-dimension.html.

[27] Coleman Barks with John Moyne, trans., *The Essential Rumi* (HarperSanFrancisco, 1995), 36.

[28] Audre Lorde, "A Litany for Survival," *The Black Unicorn: Poems* (New York: W. W. Norton, 1978), 31.

[29] Matthew 13:45-46.

[30] Liberation Theology was first articulated in 1971 by the Catholic Peruvian priest Gustavo Gutierrez, in his book, A *Theology of Liberation: History, Politics, Salvation* (1971 in Spanish, English edition Maryknoll, NY: Orbis Books, 1973).

[31] Luke 1:5, 2:1-2.

[32] Meister Eckhart (1260-1328), from "The Nobleman" in David O'Neil, ed., *Meister Eckhart, From Whom God Hid Nothing: Sermons, Writings and Sayings* (Boston: New Seeds Books 1996) 94.

[33] Mab Segrest, *Born to Belonging: Writings on Spirit and Justice* (New Brunswick, NJ: Rutgers University Press, 2002), 2.

[34] Ibid., 14.

[35] Ibid., 157-175.

[36] Matthew 25:35-40.

[37] Told by Tom Cornell, recounted in Jim Forest, *Love Is the Measure: A Biography of Dorothy Day, Founder of The Catholic Worker*, Revised Edition (Maryknoll, NY: Orbis Books), 66-67.

[38] Fyodor Dostoyevsky, *The Brothers Karamazov: A Novel in Four Parts and an Epilogue*, trans. Constance Garnett (New York: MacMillan, 1922), 53.

[39] Ibid., 55.

[40] Anthony De Mello, *The Heart of the Enlightened: A Book of Story Meditations* (New York: Image/Doubleday, 1991, 1989), 79.

[41] Dostoyevsky, 339.

[42] Thich Nhat Hanh, *The Miracle of Mindfulness*, trans. Mobi Ho (Boston: Beacon Press, 1975), 47-48.

[43] Ibid., 48.

[44] Winifred Gallagher, *Working on God* (New York: Random House, 1999), 250.

[45] Alice Walker, *The Color Purple* (New York: Harcourt, Brace, Jovanovich, 1982), 167.

[46] Ibid., 166-7.

[47] Jill Bolte Taylor, *My Stroke of Insight: A Brain Scientist's Personal Journey* (New York: Viking, 2008), 30.

[48] Linda Greenlaw, *The Hungry Ocean: A Swordboat Captain's Journey* (New York: Hyperion, 1999)

[49] Ibid., p. 249.

[50] Linda Hogan, *Dwellings*, 104.

[51] Remembered from a speech she gave in Boston, date unknown.

[52] Larry Dossey, *Healing Words: The Power of Prayer and the Practice of Medicine* (New York: HarperCollins, 1993), 7-8.

[53] Elizabeth Cunningham, "Heart Prayer," *Small Bird: Poems & Prayers* (Barrytown: Station Hill Press, 200ʊ), 9.

[54] Harvey Arden and Steve Wall, eds., *Wisdomkeepers: Meetings with Native American Spiritual Elders* (Hillsboro, OR: Beyond Words Pub., 1990), 66.

[55] http://www.citizen.org/cmep/article_redirect.cfm?ID=10304.

[56] http://www.un.org/es/comun/docs/?symbol=A/RES/64/292&lang=E.

[57] Linda Jean Shepherd, "My Life with Weed," *The Sweet Breathing of Plants: Women Writing on the Green World,* edited by Linda Hogan & Brenda Peterson (New York: North Point Press, 2001), 200.

[58] Private email, used with permission.

[59] Starhawk, *Earth Path*, 131-132.

[60] As reported in Starhawk, *Earth Path*, 152.

[61] http://www.joannamacy.net/thegreatturning/personal-guidelines-t.html

[62] Stanley Kunitz, "The Testing-Tree," *The Testing-Tree* (New York: Little Brown, 1971)

[63] See http://www.rethinkingschools.org/ProdDetails.asp?ID=094296120X

[64] See http://www.doctrineofdiscovery.org/

[65] Information from the "Motion from the Right Relationship Monitoring Committee for the UUA Board of Trustees" meeting January 2012, at http://www.doctrineofdiscovery.org/uua.docdiscovery.jan12.pdf

[66] Lewis Lord, "How Many People Were Here Before Columbus?" *U.S. News & World Report*, August 18-25, 1997, pp. 68-70. Accessed at: http://www.bxscience.edu/ourpages/auto/2009/4/5/34767803/Pre-Columbian%20population.pdf

[67] James W. Loewen, *Lies My Teacher Told Me: Everything Your American History Textbook Got Wrong* (New York: Simon & Schuster, 1995)

[68] James W. Loewen, "Plagues & Pilgrims: The Truth About the First Thanksgiving," *Rethinking Columbus*, 81.

[69] From the *Maine Wabanaki-State Child Welfare Truth and Reconciliation Commission* information pamphlet. See http://www.mainewabanakireach.org/maine_wabanaki_state_child_welfare_truth_a nd_reconciliation_commission.

[70] From the Indian Child Welfare Act, http://www.tribal-institute.org/lists/chapter21_icwa.htm.

[71] American Friends Service Committee, "Conversation with Denise Altvater on Truth and Reconciliation in Maine," at https://www.afsc.org/resource/conversation-denise-altvater-truth-and-reconciliation-maine

[72] Denise has shared her story in public forums about the Truth and Reconciliation Commission, and granted permission for me to share her story here. More information can be found about her at http://www.americanswhotellthetruth.org/portraits/denise-altvater

[73] From her talk at USM on November 15, 2012.

[74] The Commission issued its final report in June 2015. It is available at https://d3n8a8pro7vhmx.cloudfront.net/mainewabanakireach/pages/17/attachments/original/1468974047/TRC-Report-Expanded_July2015.pdf?1468974047.

[75] Linda Hogan, *Solar Storms* (New York: Scribner, 1995), 17-18.

[76] Cited in Vine Deloria, *God Is Red* (New York: Delta, 1973), 73. Quote originally comes from Luther Standing Bead, *Land of the Spotted Eagle* (Boston: Houghton Mifflin, 1933), 248.

[77] Hogan, *Solar Storms*, 228.

[78] Ibid., 235.

[79] Ibid., 236.

[80] Ibid., 240.

[81] Deloria, 75-89.

[82] Ibid., 70.

[83] Rita Nakashima Brock and Rebecca Ann Parker, *Saving Paradise: How Christianity Traded Love of This World for Crucifixion and Empire* (Boston: Beacon Press, 2008) 224.

[84] Ibid., 224-233.

[85] These ideas were explored in my essay "Wanting to Be Indian: When Spiritual Searching Turns into Cultural Theft," originally published in *The Brown Papers: a monthly essay of reflection and analysis from the Women's Theological Center*, (Boston) 1:7, April 1995.

[86] Quoted in Ward Churchill, "Spiritual Hucksterism: The Rise of the Plastic Medicine Men," in *From a Native Son: Selected Essays in Indigenism, 1985-1995* (Boston: South End Press, 1996), 357. Originally published in *Z Magazine*, Dec. 1990.

[87] "Bears need breakfast too," *The Northern Forecaster*, Falmouth, ME, July 12, 2007.

[88] Gloria Feman Orenstein, "The Shamanic Dimensions of an Ecofeminist Narrative," *The Feminist Ezine*, at http://www.feministezine.com/feminist/ecofeminism/Shamanic-Ecofeminist-Narrative.html.

[89] *Rilke's Book of Hours: Love Poems to God*, I 11, translated by Anita Barrows and Joanna Macy (New York: Riverhead Books, 1996) 57.

[90] Annie Dillard, *Teaching a Stone to Talk: Expeditions and Encounters* (New York: Harper and Row, 1982), 43.

[91] Gilbert Waldbauer, *Fireflies, Honey, and Silk* (Oakland: University of California Press, 2009), 97-98.

[92] Polly Berrien Berends, *Coming to Life: Traveling the Spiritual Path in Everyday Life*, (New York: HarperCollins, 1993), 8.

[93] Anne D. LeClaire, "Writers and... Risks," *The Cape Codder*, Nov. 3, 2000, 39.

[94] http://www.greenbeltmovement.org/who-we-are/our-history.

[95] Derrick Jensen, "Going Underground," *The Sun*, 386, February 2008, 4-11, and Paul Stamets, *Mycelium Running: How Mushrooms Can Help Save the World*, (Berkeley: Ten Speed Press, 2005).

[96] Paul Stamets, 3.

[97] Jensen, *Op. Cit.*

[98] Mykel Johnson, "Wanting to be Indian", (The Poem), *Trivia* 21, 1993, 57.

[99] Barbara Deming, "Spirit of Love," 1973, in Jane Meyerding, ed., *We Are All Part of One Another: A Barbara Deming Reader* (Philadelphia: New Society Publishers, 1984) 247.

[100] Margaret Atwood, *Survival: A Thematic Guide to Canadian Literature* (Toronto: Anansi Press, 1972).

[101] "The God Who Only Knows Four Words," *The Gift: Poems by Hafiz, The Great Sufi Master*, Translations by Daniel Ladinsky, (New York: Penguin, 1999) 270.

[102] http://africa.mountmadonnaschool.org/2012/09/27/angeles-arrien-dancer-in-the-toll-booth/.

[103] Joanna Macy, http://www.joannamacy.net/thegreatturning.html.

[104] David C. Korten, *The Great Turning: From Empire to Earth Community* (San Franciso: People-Centered Development Forum/ Berrett-Koehler Publishers, 2006), 74-75. Referring to the work of John Feltwell, *The Natural History of Butterflies*

(New York: Facts on File, 1986), 23, and Elisabet Sahtouris, *EarthDance: Living Systems in Evolution* (San Jose, CA: iUniversity Press, 2000).

[105] Parker Palmer, interview by Sarah Ruth van Gelder, "Integral Life, Integral Teacher," in *Yes! A Journal of Positive Futures*, Winter 1999, http://www.yesmagazine.org/issues/education-for-life/796.

[106] Korton, *The Great Turning*, 84-85.

[107] "I See the Promised Land", *A Testament of Hope: The Essential Writings and Speeches of Martin Luther King, Jr.*, James M. Washington, ed. (Harper Collins, 1986), 286.

[108] Ibid., p. 286.

[109] Mark Twain, *Following the Equator: A Journey Around the World* (Hartford: American Publishing Co., 1897), 348.

[110] My thanks to Kathy Lilly for her kind permission to share this story in a sermon many years ago.

[111] Dave Carter, *The Mountain*, copyright David Robert Carter, 2000, recorded on the album *Tanglewood Tree*, Dave Carter & Tracy Grammer, 2002.

[112] Wendell Berry, *The Unforeseen Wilderness: Kentucky's Red River Gorge* (Berkeley: North Point Press, 1991, revised & expanded version), 43.

Made in the USA
Middletown, DE
03 June 2022

66612431R00109